Indiana Employer's Guide to Wage and Hour Issues

Published by:

Indiana Chamber
115 W. Washington Street, Suite 850 S
PO Box 44926
Indianapolis, IN 46244-0926
(317) 264-3110
www.indianachamber.com

Authored by:

Ice Miller
One American Square, Box 82001
Indianapolis, IN 46282-002
(317) 236-2100
www.icemiller.com

Published by

The Voice of
Indiana Business.

Layout/Design: Danielle Beck
Editor: Indiana Chamber
Cover Design: Tony Spataro
Printing: Midland Press Corp

115 W. Washington St., Suite 850 S
PO Box 44926
Indianapolis, IN 46244-0926
www.indianachamber.com

The information compiled in this handbook is being provided by the Indiana
Chamber as a service to the business community. Although every effort has been
made to ensure the accuracy and completeness of this information, the Indiana
Chamber and the authors and reviewers of the publication cannot be responsible for
any errors and omissions, nor any agency's interpretations, applications and
changes of regulations described herein.

This publication is designed to provide accurate and authoritative information in a
highly summarized manner with regard to the subject matter covered. The contents
are intended for general information purposes only. The information in this
publication is subject to constant change and therefore should serve only as a
foundation for further investigation and study. It is sold with the understanding
that the publisher and others associated with this publication are not engaged in
rendering legal, technical, or other professional service on any specific fact or
circumstances. Neither the authors nor the Indiana Chamber make any
representation that adherence to the subject matter herein will be considered
adequate compliance with wage and hour laws and regulations as interpreted by the
courts or federal or state agencies charged with the enforcement of such laws and
regulations. The contents are intended for general information only. You are urged
to consult your own attorney or other technical specialist concerning your own
situation and any specific legal or technical questions you may have.

This publication is available from:

Indiana Chamber of Commerce
115 W. Washington St., Suite 850 S
Indianapolis, IN 46204
(317) 264-6885

ISBN 1-883698-47-2

Price: $85 per copy plus tax and shipping. For information on volume discounts and
consignment, or distribution arrangements, contact Customer Service at the Indiana
Chamber, at (800) 824-6885.

Dear Reader,

Ice Miller is pleased to join with the Indiana Chamber of Commerce to provide the *Indiana Employer's Guide to Wage and Hour Issues*. Multi-million dollar verdicts for unpaid overtime and hours worked "off the clock" have been splashed across the front page in recent months, and as this law has become more familiar to the general public (and plaintiff's bar in particular), claims under the Fair Labor Standards Act have become a staple of employment litigation.

This handbook will provide the reader with an overview of the basic requirements of wage and hour laws, and several other laws related to wage payments and deductions, together with numerous examples and forms to serve as a practical guide in complying with these complex laws. However, this handbook is only a starting point. When a possible problem has been identified (*e.g.*, whether a particular incentive payment must be included in calculating overtime) a careful and thorough review of the facts and law is required to produce a safe, effective compliance strategy. In some cases (such as the "percentage of wage bonus") a method may be available to accomplish the desired result and fully comply at the same time.

One of the most important preventive services offered by Ice Miller is the wage and hour compliance audit. This procedure helps our clients identify and correct potential wage and hour problems before they reach the level of a dispute. We also assist our clients in drafting and implementing payroll and employment policies that comply with the many wage and hour laws. If a client is charged with violating one of these laws, Ice Miller provides experienced, well-informed counsel to represent our client in a vigorous defense of its position.

In addition to wage and hour issues, Ice Miller can also assist with the entire range of labor and employment issues, such as:

- Employment Litigation
- Employment Agreements
- OSHA
- FMLA
- ADA
- Immigration
- Union Activity and Organization Efforts

We believe, from the introduction to the last chapter (a state-of-the-art review of child support and garnishment requirements), this guidebook will provide a user-friendly source of reference to you and other business readers in understanding and satisfying the demands of wage and hour laws.

Sincerely,

Ice Miller
Labor and Employment Section

LEGAL & BUSINESS ADVISORS

FIRM OVERVIEW

Founded in 1910, Ice Miller is the largest law firm in Indianapolis with a nationally recognized reputation in many of its practice areas. With additional offices in Chicago and Washington D.C., the firm has over 225 lawyers, 40 paraprofessionals and 250 support staff members. Ice Miller is a full-service firm with the resources it needs to counsel its clients and deliver quality legal and business advice.

Ice Miller offers a broad array of capabilities in virtually all areas of the legal practice. The firm's broad practice areas include business, employment and labor law, litigation, public finance and real estate. Our dedication to maintaining and growing a wide range of more discrete practice areas enables us to identify options and offer the legal assistance needed to address clients' needs creatively.

Our firm was founded on a commitment to provide personal service and valued legal counsel to our clients. After almost 90 years, that hasn't changed. We cultivate close working partnerships between clients and attorneys to ensure personal attention is provided every step of the way. And we clearly establish who has overall responsibility for the work performed on each matter — you are assured of well-managed, cost-effective and timely service under the supervision of your relationship partner.

Staying on top of legal and business changes is an important part of our service. We have seasoned partners who have been involved in many of the most important legal matters in the country. These partners pass on their knowledge and perspective to our associates who are leading graduates of our nation's top law schools. Our commitment to ongoing legal education and training, supervision, peer review and total quality creates a forward-thinking environment that benefits all of our clients.

We believe that rapid information retrieval and sharing is a critical component of excellent client service. Our technology professionals provide firm personnel with the computer and communications systems needed to expedite the delivery of services, in the office or on the road. From our computerized law library and advanced telecommunications systems, our lawyers are connected and accessible.

We also recognize that flexible attorney-client fee arrangements and cost control are a part of the partnership between the client and our firm. We will work with you to tailor our services to meet your financial needs.

	Wayne "Skip" O. Adams III (317) 236-2117 wayne.adams@icemiller.com		**Kerry S. Martin** (317) 236-5957 kerry.martin@icemiller.com
	Michael A. Blickman (317) 236-2298 michael.blickman@icemiller.com		**Byron L. Myers** (317) 236-2367 byron.myers@icemiller.com
	Michael H. Boldt (317) 236-2327 michael.boldt@icemiller.com		**Richard E. Parker** (317) 236-2314 richard.parker@icemiller.com
	Samuel "Chic" Roydon Born II (317) 236-2305 samuel.born@icemiller.com		**Steven F. Pockrass** (317) 236-5921 steven.pockrass@icemiller.com
	Jenifer M. Brown (317) 236-2242 jenifer.brown@icemiller.com		**William R. Riggs** (317) 236-2273 william.riggs@icemiller.com
	David J. Carr (317) 236-5840 david.carr@icemiller.com		**Eric C. Scroggins** (317) 236-5887 eric.scroggins@icemiller.com
	Tami A. Earnhart (317) 236-2235 tami.earnhart@icemiller.com		**Kathleen K. Shortridge** (317) 236-2495 kathleen.shortridge@icemiller.com
	Mark Wilson Ford (317) 236-2366 mark.ford@icemiller.com		**Paul Harrison Sinclair** (317) 236-2176 paul.sinclair@icemiller.com
	Pamela V. Keller (317) 236-5868 Pamela.Keller@icemiller.com		**Susan Beidler Tabler** (317) 236-2301 susan.tabler@icemiller.com
	Martin Jay Klaper (317) 236-2322 martin.klaper@icemiller.com		**Michael L. Tooley** (317) 236-2118 michael.tooley@icemiller.com

Workforce problems aren't always this easy to spot, or to fix.

Your human resources are certainly your most valuable ones, and by far your most complex. Issues with those resources can range from the obvious to the insidious. From the executive suite to the factory floor. All can hurt you. All can be helped.

That's where we come in.

From human resource concerns, to work environment issues, to contracts and executive compensation and incentive needs, we bring experience, empathy and insight to workforce management. We know your industry. We know your business. We know the law. And we know people.

At Ice Miller, we have that insight, along with the resource depth and diversity to take on a problem you're facing and bring it to resolution. Efficiently and effectively.

Workforce and workplace services:
Wage and Hour Issues • Dispute resolution
Corporate risk management and compliance strategies
Organized labor issues • Contract negotiation
Employee benefits • Executive compensation and incentives

ICEMILLER ®
LEGAL & BUSINESS ADVISORS

It's a complex world. Be advised.

Preface

If you have employees and a payroll, then I don't need to tell you how complex and confusing wage and hour issues can be, even if you deal with them on a daily basis. There are many responsibilities and requirements that employers must understand and comply with, beginning with the Fair Labor Standards Act. And, with the recent Indiana Supreme Court case upholding the award of treble damages and attorney's fees in a case in which wages owed were not timely paid, it can be very costly to not fully understand and comply with these laws. Take it from someone who has practiced law for over 30 years, these laws were not written to be easily understood. In order to assist Indiana employers in your compliance efforts, the Indiana Chamber of Commerce and the law firm of Ice Miller have collaborated to bring you this new edition of the *Indiana Employer's Guide to Wage & Hour Issues.*

The purpose of this handbook is to provide employers with practical, concise and easy-to-understand advice and assistance. If, however, after looking through the handbook, you can't find the answer or you just want a second opinion, then, if you are a member of the Indiana Chamber of Commerce, please feel free to give me a call and I will assist you with your issue.

George Raymond
Vice President, Human Resources, Labor Relations and Civil Justice

George Raymond joined the Indiana Chamber of Commerce in October 1999. He is responsible for issues concerning human resources, unemployment and worker's compensation insurance, general employee and labor matters, and civil justice.

George spent 30 years with Amax Coal Company and its successor companies, holding a variety of legal and management positions. Most recently, George served as national director of land management and governmental relations for Cyprus Amax Minerals Company, headquartered in Denver, Colorado.

George is a graduate of Purdue University and obtained his law and MBA degrees from Indiana University.

Along with other Chamber lobbyists, George Raymond seeks the enactment of appropriate legislation to enhance the viability of business in Indiana. He, along with the other Indiana Chamber lobbyists, works hard to defeat measures that would restrict an employer's rights and drive up business costs.

Table of Contents

Chapter 1

Introduction

The purpose of this handbook is to assist employers in navigating the labyrinth of state and federal wage and hour laws confronting Indiana employers. Federal and state wage and hour law presents a panoply of traps for the unwary. From nurses to golf course grounds keeping crews to Christmas wreath-makers, wage and hour law offers something for everybody. Perhaps no area of labor and employment law presents such stark examples of the gory aftermath of legislative compromise. Yet, do not despair. This handbook represents the Indiana Chamber of Commerce's best effort to assist you in avoiding the dubious distinction of being the next "test case" in this difficult and dangerous area of law.

In the beginning there was the laborer, toiling all day long in the field, or perhaps hunting the woolly mammoth for its food and hide (first known example of the "piece worker?"), or working at some other basic task for which the poor soul hoped for recompense. With the advent of the industrial revolution, employers determined that capital could be accumulated by convincing employees to work for the employer for as long and as hard as possible, and if children could be drawn into the workplace, their labor could prove even more profitable.

By the commencement of the 20th century, a host of adverse workplace conditions reached the attention of Congress. However, only in the throes of the Great Depression did Congress enact the Fair Labor Standards Act (FLSA). A widely held view suggests that the real justification for the FLSA was not to protect employees so much as it was to spur employment, by penalizing employers who worked their employees more than 40 hours per week. The notion was that this would create an incentive for employers to hire new workers, thus reducing the staggering unemployment levels and help pull the country out of economic despair.

Whatever its genesis, the FLSA provided for the establishment of fair labor standards in employment for those employers who could be regulated by virtue of their connection to interstate commerce. It regulates both the hours and wages of employees. Specifically, the FLSA places a floor under wages by establishing a nationwide minimum wage, and it places a penetrable ceiling over hours of employment by requiring overtime compensation for hours worked over 40 each week. Significantly, regulated employers must also comply with state and local wage hour laws; the FLSA does not pre-empt any state or local laws applicable to wages and hours. The FLSA also restricts the use of child labor, and weighs in on the issue of "equal pay" between men and women who perform "substantially similar" jobs.

The FLSA's coverage is exceptionally broad, and the U.S. Supreme Court has ruled that it should be liberally construed. Yet, a number of wage-related issues are not directly regulated by the FLSA. These include vacation pay, holiday pay, severance pay, sick pay, premium pay for weekend or holiday work, pay raises and fringe benefits. A number of these issues are separately addressed by Indiana state law, and are described in Chapter 5.

Although Indiana has laws that govern minimum wage and overtime requirements, these laws do not apply to any employee that is covered by the FLSA. Thus, while under the FLSA states are capable of providing more generous rules for wages and hours than those set forth under the FLSA, Indiana has taken the approach that its minimum wage and overtime laws only apply to those few and very small local employers who would not be covered under the FLSA. The Indiana minimum wage is currently the same as the federal minimum wage, $5.15 per hour as of February 2004, and Indiana imposes the same overtime requirement as the FLSA; however, the Indiana minimum wage has historically lagged behind the FLSA and may do so in the future if the federal minimum wage is increased. Perhaps, more significantly, Indiana also possesses its own state child labor laws, which impose meaningful restrictions that go beyond the requirements of the federal law, and which are discussed in Chapter 8.

Federal contractors face an additional gauntlet through which to run if they wish to avoid violation of the wage-hour laws. The Walsh-Healy Public

Contracts Act, the Davis-Bacon Act and the Service Contract Act of 1965 all require the attention of federal contractors. These are discussed in Chapter 10.

Chapter 2

Coverage Under the FLSA

Overview

The Fair Labor Standards Act has the broadest possible coverage, based on the constitutional power of the federal government to regulate interstate commerce. Almost all employees are covered by the provisions of the FLSA. It is a difficult and risky proposition to deny coverage, and even if a plausible argument can be maintained, the basis for non-coverage must be reviewed on a weekly basis and could easily change as a business grows and increases its interstate character. In this chapter, we first assume that an individual is an "employee" of an "employer" and we explore the issue of coverage, which is based on either the individual's or the employer's involvement in interstate commerce. Then, we discuss the situation in which an individual might not be considered "employed" in the first place, including the status of employees of "independent contractors," and the concept of "joint employment," employment in separate jobs within a single enterprise and the use of volunteers or interns.

Individual Employee Coverage

As initially enacted, the FLSA based its coverage on the activities of employees, without regard to the activity of the employers. This original basis of coverage was called "individual" or "traditional" coverage. The Act was amended by Congress in 1962 to add "enterprise coverage" (described below), which provides coverage based on the activities of the employer, rather than those of the individual employees. Although enterprise coverage now controls most coverage issues, individual employee coverage remains an issue for employers whose annual dollar volume takes them below the threshold for enterprise coverage (currently at $500,000).

An employee is individually covered by the FLSA, regardless of the status of his or her employer, if he or she is engaged in (a) interstate or foreign commerce; or (b) the production of goods for transportation, including fringe production activities. Commerce for the purposes of these categories is defined as trade, commerce, transportation, transmission or communication among the states, or between any state and any place outside that state.

Employees are considered to be engaged in interstate commerce for the purpose of determining individual coverage if they:

- operate instrumentalities of commerce (roads, bridges, airports);

- transport goods across state lines;

- regularly cross state lines in the course of their work; use channels of interstate commerce in the course of their duties (including media, banking, insurance, etc.); or

- regularly communicate across state lines.

Employees considered to be involved in the production of goods for transportation include employees involved in manufacturing, mining, handling, transporting or other activities related to the production of goods to be sold across state lines, whether as finished products or as components of other products.

In order to fall within the first category of individual coverage, an employee's activities in interstate or foreign commerce must be regular and recurring, as opposed to isolated, sporadic or occasional. There is, however, no precise test for examining how much of the employee's time, or what percentage of that time, is spent in activities related to interstate or foreign commerce. If an employee is engaged in commerce on a regular and recurring basis, he or she will be individually covered even if the amount of time spent in such activities is relatively small.

Coverage under the individual employee test is not limited to employees working pursuant to an hourly wage rate, but applies as well to employees paid on a piecework, salary, commission or other basis. In addition, coverage is not dependent on the location where the work is performed, meaning that individuals may be covered whether they perform their work at home, in a factory or office, or elsewhere.

It is important to underscore that an employee does not forfeit coverage under the individual coverage test merely by performing some activities that are not covered in and of themselves. If, for example, an employee who is not otherwise exempt from the FLSA engages in covered and non-covered activities during the same workweek, that employee would be entitled to the FLSA benefits for all of the time worked during that week, not just the covered portion. Wage benefits under the FLSA are determined on a workweek basis, and courts will not attempt to segregate between covered and non-covered work performed by an employee during the same workweek.

Enterprise Coverage

Employees who do not qualify for coverage under the individual employee test based on the nature of their own work still may be covered under the FLSA due to the nature of their employer's business. This is known as the "enterprise basis" for coverage and covers virtually every business that grosses $500,000 or more in sales or business on an annual basis. A worker employed by a business determined to be an enterprise is subject to all the benefits and rights afforded under the FLSA just as though the employee qualified under the individual employee coverage test described above, unless an exemption applies.

A business will be considered an enterprise covered by the FLSA if it has two or more employees and is one of the following:

- Establishments of any type which employ two or more individuals who are engaged in commerce or the production of goods for commerce, or has employees handling, selling or otherwise working on goods or materials that have been moved in or produced for commerce by any person, and has an gross volume of sales or business of $500,000 or more (not counting excise taxes at the retail level). This definition includes all those who would be covered under the two prongs of the individual coverage test discussed above, but also those who are only "handling" goods that have moved in commerce, a much more inclusive category. It is a rare business indeed that can successfully assert that not more than one of its employees "handles" goods which have moved in interstate commerce.

- Establishments engaged in the operation of a hospital, an institution primarily engaged in the care of the sick, the aged or the mentally ill who reside on the premises; a school for mentally or physically disabled or gifted children; a preschool, an elementary or secondary school, or an institution of higher education (whether operated for profit or not for profit).

- Activities of a public agency, whether at the local, state or federal level.

There is an exclusion from the enterprise coverage test for establishments whose only regular employees are the owner or persons standing in the relationship of parent, spouse, child or other member of the immediate family of the owner. These establishments are commonly referred to as "mom and pop" businesses, and will not lose the benefit of the exclusion merely by the sporadic or irregular employment of non-family members.

> **Example.** Mike's Southern Kitchen on the Indianapolis south side employs a manager, a cook and three part-time servers, in addition to Mike, the owner. Although Mike boasts of authentic southern style cooking, Mike in fact buys all his food and other supplies himself, at a local market. His restaurant serves lunches for employees at nearby businesses, all of which are sold and consumed on location. None of his employees use the mail or telephone in connection with their work. Total gross revenue for Mike's business is less than $500,000 per year. At present, Mike's employees are not covered by the FLSA, because they are not individually engaged in interstate commerce, and Mike's business is not covered as an enterprise. (They are all covered by the Indiana state minimum wage and overtime provisions.)

> However, the business receives an unsolicited call from an out-of-state supplier, who offers Mike a better deal on paper supplies and cleaning equipment. Since the supplier is from Louisville, Mike is receptive and he places the first order on the phone. From then on, the manager and cook use the telephone to order supplies from this supplier once or twice each month, relieving Mike of the burden of having to make an extra stop in town to pick up these items. Those two employees are now covered by the FLSA, since they are engaged in interstate commerce. And all of Mike's employees may

soon be covered, based on enterprise coverage, if the business grows to over $500,000 per year.

Independent Contractors

The FLSA is intended to apply to "employees" of covered employers and not to others who may provide services to those employers outside the context of an employment relationship, such as independent contractors and consultants. The distinction between employees and these other categories of service providers has come under increased scrutiny in the recent years, as many individuals have become interested in pursuing non-traditional career paths and employers in many industries have looked for ways to increase their flexibility (and lower their employment costs) through the use of creative working arrangements.

As with many areas of employment law, labels are helpful but not controlling in determining whether a relationship can properly be classified as an employer-employee relationship or an independent contractor relationship. A number of large employers have been hit with lawsuits under the FLSA, ERISA and other laws alleging that they mislabeled individuals as independent contractors for the purpose of avoiding their obligation to pay overtime or allow the individuals to participate in benefit plans available to employees. As these employers will attest, the consequences of misclassifying such individuals can be costly.

Who's Who: Separating Employees from Independent Contractors

Factors Considered by Courts

In determining whether an individual is an employee or an independent contractor (or some other label) under the FLSA, the Department of Labor and the courts use a version of the "duck" test -- if it looks like a duck, waddles like a duck and quacks like a duck, it will be presumed to be a duck! In other words, the courts look at whether, as a matter of "economic reality," the individual is economically dependent on the business of the entity to whom he or she is providing services, or whether the individual is actually in business for himself or herself.

The primary factor considered by courts focuses on who has the *right to control* the methods and means of the worker's performance. A worker is generally considered to be an employee if the entity or person for whom the services are provided has the right of control over the methods and means of the worker's performance, even if the control is not regularly exercised. Conversely, if the worker retains control over the methods and means by which he or she performs the work, courts generally will consider the worker to be an independent contractor.

Other factors considered by courts include:

- the duration and permanency of the relationship;

- the skill required for the task (with more specialized skills leading to an inference that the worker is an independent contractor);

- the investment of the worker in the equipment, materials and facilities required for the work;

- the opportunity for profit or loss by the worker;

- the amount of initiative, judgment or foresight required for the allegedly independent enterprise to succeed in competition with others.

In a 1992 decision, the Supreme Court looked at all of these factors, stating that "all incidents of the relationship must be assessed with no one factor being decisive."

The Internal Revenue Service Test

In addition to the common-law factors described above, courts will look to a revenue ruling issued by the Internal Revenue Service (IRS), which has a more elaborate and more often used framework spelling out how that agency determines employment status for tax purposes. In classifying a worker as either an independent contractor or employee under this ruling, the IRS balances 20 factors that tend to demonstrate whether the business has the authority to direct and control the manner in which the worker performs his or her duties. The greater the control by the business, the more likely that the worker will be treated as an employee. The 20 factors examined by the IRS include the following:

- **Instructions.** A worker who is required to comply with the company's instructions about when, where and how he or she is to work is ordinarily an employee. This control factor is present if the company for whom the services are performed has the "right" to require compliance with instructions (even if the company does not exercise that right).

- **Training.** A worker who is trained by an employer or attends training sessions is ordinarily an employee.

- **Integration.** Integration of the worker's services into the business operations generally shows that the work is subject to the company's direction and control. When the success or continuation of a business depends to an appreciable degree upon the performance of certain services, the workers who perform those services are typically employees.

- **Services rendered personally.** If the services must be rendered by the worker personally, the worker is typically an employee because the company for whom the services are performed is interested in the methods used to accomplish the work as well as the results.

- **Hiring, supervising and paying assistants.** In the event that the worker hires, supervises and pays its own assistants (as opposed to relying on the company's employees or assistants), the worker resembles an independent contractor.

- **Continuing relationship.** A continuing relationship between the worker and the company for whom the services are performed indicates that an employment relationship exists. A continuing relationship may exist where work is performed at frequently recurring although irregular intervals.

- **Set hours of work.** Where the worker is required to be present for and perform services during set hours of work, the relationship appears as an employment relationship.

- **Full-time.** If the worker must devote substantially full-time to the business of the company for whom the services are performed, the worker resembles an employee. An independent contractor, on the other hand, is free to work when and for whom he or she chooses.

- **Doing work on employer's premises.** If the work is performed on the premises of the company for whom the services are performed, this factor suggests control over the worker, especially if the work could be done elsewhere.

- **Order or sequence set.** If a worker must perform services in the order or sequence set by the company for whom the services are performed, this factor indicates or suggests an employment relationship. If the worker retains the right to determine the order or sequence of work, the worker resembles an independent contractor.

- **Oral or written reports.** A requirement that the worker submit regular oral or written reports to the company for whom the services are performed indicates an employment relationship.

- **Payment by hour, week or month.** Payment by the hour, week or month generally suggests an employment relationship, provided that this method of payment is not just a convenient way of paying a lump sum agreed upon as the cost of a job. Payment made by the job or on a straight commission generally indicates that the worker is an independent contractor.

- **Payment of business and/or traveling expenses.** If the company for whom the services are performed pays the worker's business and/or traveling expenses, the worker is ordinarily an employee. An employer, to be able to control expenses, generally retains the right to regulate and direct the worker's business activities.

- **Furnishing of tools and materials.** Where a worker furnishes significant tools, materials and other equipment, this factor generally indicates that the worker is an independent contractor.

- **Significant investment.** If the worker invests in facilities that are used by the worker in performing services and are not typically maintained by employees (such as the maintenance of an office), this factor tends to indicate that the worker is an independent contractor. On the other hand, lack of investment in facilities indicates dependence on the company for whom the services are performed and, accordingly, the existence of an employment relationship.

- **Realization of profit or loss.** A worker who can realize a profit or suffer a loss as a result of the worker's services (in addition to the profit or loss ordinarily realized by employees) is generally an independent contractor.

- **Working for more than one firm at a time.** If a worker performs more than de minimis services for a multiple of unrelated persons or firms, this factor generally indicates that the worker is an independent contractor.

- **Making services available to the general public.** The fact that a worker makes his or her services available to the general public on a regular and consistent basis indicates an independent contractor relationship.

- **Right to discharge.** The right to discharge a worker is a factor indicating that the worker is an employee and the person possessing the right is an employer. An employer exercises control through the threat of dismissal, which causes the worker to obey the employer's instructions. An independent contractor, on the other hand, cannot be fired so long as the independent contractor produces a result that meets the contract specifications.

- **Right to terminate.** If the worker has the right to end his or her relationship with the company for whom the services are performed at any time he or she wishes without incurring liability, this factor indicates an employment relationship.

In 1996, the IRS modified its approach to the issue of classifying a worker as either an independent contractor or an employee. While the IRS did not abandon the 20-factor test, it did refocus its approach to this issue by stating that the "most persuasive evidence" on the issue of classification relates to the following three broad categories of information:

- **Behavioral control.** This factor focuses on whether there is a right to direct or control how the work is done. The presence or absence of instructions and training on how work is to be done is especially relevant.

- **Financial control.** This factor focuses on whether there is a right to direct or control how the business aspects of the worker's activities are conducted. Specifically, the IRS will look for significant investments by the worker, unreimbursed expenses, services available to the relevant market, method of payment and opportunity for profit or loss.

- **Relationship of the parties.** This factor focuses on how the parties perceive their relationship. When assessing this factor, the IRS will look to the intent of the parties, any written contracts or agreements, employee benefits, terms of discharge/termination, the permanency of the relationship and the regular business activities of the company.

Practical Considerations

The classification of workers as either independent contractors or employees is extremely fact sensitive and may change from time to time. Businesses that are concerned with preserving independent contractor relationships with their service providers should regularly measure those relationships against the factors described above to ensure that the service providers actually are functioning as independent contractors. Also, businesses should consider entering into written agreements at the outset of the relationship that underscore the parties' intent that the relationship be that of an independent contractor rather than employer-employee, and which require the independent contractor to comply with all wage and hours laws (specifically listed) and indemnify the principle from liability for non-compliance.

Joint Employment

Another issue that comes up from time to time relates to how employees will be treated under the FLSA when they perform work for two different employers during the same workweek. This issue frequently arises in the temporary employee or employee leasing context, in which a leasing agency provides employees to businesses to perform work on the premises of those businesses. The fact that a leasing agency is an independent contractor does not relieve the principle employer from liability if the employees are considered jointly employed by both.

The Department of Labor has promulgated regulations that provide that, where the employee performs work that simultaneously benefits two or more employers, or where the employee works for two or more employers at different times during the workweek, a joint employment relationship will be considered to exist under any one of the following situations:

- Where there is an arrangement between the employers to share the employee's services – for example, to interchange employees.

- Where one employer is acting directly or indirectly in the interest of the other employer (or employers) in relation to the employee.

- Where the employers are not completely disassociated with respect to the employment of a particular employee and may be deemed to share control of the employee, directly or indirectly, by reason of the fact that one employer controls, is controlled by or is under common control with the other employer.

Where an application of these factors establishes that the two employers constitute one business entity with respect to the employees of the business, the total number of hours worked by the employee for both employers must be added together in determining whether the employee exceeds the weekly 40-hour-per-workweek standard. In addition, both employers may be held jointly and severally liable for paying any overtime payments that are due.

Single Enterprise Test

In addition to the DOL factors described above, courts have also developed a separate test for determining whether related businesses should be treated as a "single enterprise" for purposes of the FLSA. Just as under the joint employment theory, if courts determine that two businesses function as a single enterprise, then all of the hours worked by the employees who may work for both businesses will be added together in determining overtime payments.

Two companies constitute a "single enterprise" within the meaning of the FLSA when the companies perform related activities; under unified operations or common control; and for a common business purpose. The activities of two companies are "related" if they are the same or similar, or if they are "auxiliary and service activities," such as bookkeeping, purchasing or advertising. The critical inquiry is whether there is "operational interdependence" between the two entities. Entities which provide mutually supportive services to the substantial advantage of each entity are operationally interdependent and may be treated as a single enterprise under the Act.

If the activities of the two companies are related, the question then becomes whether the operations are unified or under common control. "Unified operations" occur when two entities combine, unite or organize the performance of the related activities so that the two entities "are in effect a single business unit or an organized business system that is an economic unit directed to the accomplishment of a common business purpose." The operations are under common control when the power to "direct, restrict, regulate, govern, or administer the performance" of the related activities is "controlled by one person or by a number of persons, corporations, or other organizational units acting together." While ownership may be an important factor in determining common control, the focus of the inquiry is the *performance* of the related activities.

Assuming the companies engage in related activities and have either unified operations or common control, the final question is whether the companies operate for a common business purpose. The term "common business purpose" generally encompasses activities "which are directed to the same business objective or to similar objectives in which the group has an interest."

The determination of whether a joint employment relationship or single enterprise exists is extremely fact sensitive. Employers with concerns about whether such relationship may exist should contact experienced wage and hour counsel.

Volunteers

Definition of a Volunteer

Notwithstanding the notoriety and questionable duties of one particular White House "intern" during a recent presidential administration, the use of unpaid interns and other volunteers has skyrocketed in recent years. A volunteer is generally defined as an individual who performs hours of service for a public agency for civic, charitable, religious or humanitarian reasons, usually on a part-time basis. Examples include:

- high school or college students who intern with government or business to gain experience and often to earn academic credit;

- members of civic organizations who help out in a sheltered workshop;

- church groups who provide personal services to organizations that care for the sick, elderly or disadvantaged youths; and

- parents who assist in the school cafeteria or library.

If such services are performed without promise, expectation or receipt of compensation, the individual will not be considered an employee of the organizations that receive their service and will not be subject to the FLSA.

Other factors considered by the Department of Labor include whether the volunteer is performing work which would otherwise be performed by a regular employee and whether the employer derives any immediate advantage from the activities by the volunteers. The activities of mentally or physically disabled volunteers, who are extensively working for therapeutic purposes, but who are performing the normal function otherwise performed by employees for the direct benefit of the employer have raised difficult issues, and in several instances have been held to constitute employment.

Permitted Payments and Benefits to Volunteers

Although volunteers are generally unpaid, the FLSA permits them to be reimbursed for expenses, reasonable benefits and nominal fees, without destroying their status as volunteers. An example of such reimbursable expenses would be:

- a uniform allowance or reimbursement for cleaning expenses for a school crossing guard, or

- out-of-pocket expenses incurred during volunteering, such as meals and transportation.

A volunteer may also be reimbursed for tuition, transportation and meal costs involved in attending classes in which the purpose is to teach the volunteers to perform the services they provide or will provide as volunteer. Volunteer may also be furnished with books and supplies essential to their training.

Illegal Aliens Covered by FLSA

The courts have determined that undocumented/falsely documented (illegal) aliens who are employed (knowingly or unknowingly) by an employer are covered by the minimum wage and overtime provisions of the FLSA, since such coverage reduces the incentive to hire illegal workers by assuring that wages and employment conditions of lawful residents are not adversely affected by competition from illegal alien employees. Thus, an employer can be found liable for failure to pay minimum wage or overtime as required in the FLSA, even though it is determined in the course of an audit that the claimant was not authorized to work in the U.S. (and even if the alien lied to and presented false documents to the employer).

An employer may also be liable for civil or criminal penalties for failure to properly complete I-9 verification, and/or for knowingly employing or continuing to employ any foreign national who does not have lawful authorization to work in the U.S. However, if the employer was presented documents that appeared genuine, completed the I-9 employment verification and was unaware of the alien's unauthorized status, the employer would not be subject to sanctions.

Chapter 3
Exemptions

Although the vast majority of employers and employees are covered by the FLSA, many employees are "exempt" from the minimum wage and/or overtime requirements. The appropriate determination by the employer as to whether a particular employee is exempt is critical. The wrong conclusion can lead to significant exposure for failure to pay overtime, which is the most common reason for lawsuits filed against employers under the FLSA.

Employers commonly make two types of mistakes which lead to employees being improperly classified as an exempt employee. First, some employers incorrectly equate the terms "salaried employee" and "exempt." The fact that an employer elects to pay an employee on a salaried basis <u>does not</u> mean that the employee is therefore exempt from the overtime compensation requirements of the FLSA. A second common error by employers is misclassification of an employee as exempt based on the employee's job title and/or job description. An employee's job title and job description is all but irrelevant to the analysis of whether the employee is exempt versus not exempt. It is the duties and responsibilities actually performed by the employee which govern the determination.

The most significant and widely used exemptions are the "white collar" exemptions allowed for Executive (supervisory), Administrative, and Professional employees and the exemptions for outside sales and computer employees. These exemptions and the most recently issued regulations governing operation of the exemptions effective August 23, 2004, are discussed below.

White Collar Exemptions

The "white collar" exemptions for executive, administrative, and professional employees share two basic requirements:

- The employee's "primary duty" must be the performance of work of an exempt nature.

- The employee must be paid on a "salary or fee basis" which means a method of payment not subject to reduction because of variations in number of hours worked or in the quality of work performed. The salary must be at least $455 per week.

An employer is NOT required to treat an employee as exempt, even if the employee's actual job duties do clearly qualify for exemption. Whether to utilize an exemption is a matter of employer discretion. It is not a violation of the law to pay an "exempt" employee an hourly rate only for hours worked as long as the hourly rate exceeds the minimum wage and the "exempt" employee is paid time and one-half (1½) for hours worked over 40 in a work week. An otherwise "exempt" employee who regularly works part-time (fewer than 40 hours each week) and is not paid at least $455 per week, regardless of the hours worked that week, is not "exempt." Records of hours worked by such part-time "exempt" workers must be maintained since they are in reality non-exempt.

Defining the Executive Exemption

To qualify as an exempt executive, an employee has to meet the salary test ($455 a week or more) and:

- The employee's "primary duty" consists of the management of the enterprise, or a customarily recognized department or subdivision of the business; and the employee

- "Customarily and regularly" directs the work of two or more full time employees or their equivalent; and the employee

- Has the authority to hire or fire other employees or the employee's suggestions and recommendations as to hiring, firing, advancement, promotion or other change of status of other employees are given "particular weight."

"Primary duty" refers to the "principal, main, major, or most important duty the employee performs" <u>rather than the percentage</u> of time the employee spends performing that duty. The focus of the analysis is on the character of the employee's job as a whole. This means that managers who spend much or most of every workday working shoulder-to-shoulder with staff (such as restaurant managers) should be found to be exempt if their primary duty is to oversee operations and direct personnel.

Factors for employers to consider when determining an employee's primary duty include the relative importance of the exempt duties as compared with other types of duties; the amount of time spent performing exempt work; the employee's relative freedom from direct supervision; and the relationship between the employee's salary and the wages paid to other employees for the kind of nonexempt work performed by the employee. While employees who spend more than 50 percent of their time performing exempt work generally satisfy the primary duty requirement, time alone is not the sole test in determining a worker's primary duty.

"Customarily and regularly" means a frequency greater than occasional but less than constant, *i.e.* recurrently.

"Two or more employees" means two or more full-time employees or their equivalent, such as one full-time (40 hours or more each week) employee and two part-time employees who together work 40 hours per week.

"Particular Weight" goes to the question as to whether it is part of the employee's job duties to make such recommendations or suggestions; the frequency with which they are made or are requested to be made; and the frequency with which they are relied upon.

Executive Equity Owners

An additional category of exempt executives are those persons who own at least a 20 percent equity interest in a business if they also are actively engaged in managing that business. There is no salary test requirement for these executives.

Defining the Administrative Exemption

Employees are exempt under the administrative exemption if, in addition to meeting the $455 a week minimum salary requirement, they have as their "primary duty" the performance of office or non-manual work which (1) is "directly related" to the employer's management policies or general business operations of the employer or the employer's customers and (2) requires the exercise of "discretion and independent judgment with respect to matters of significance."

- "Primary duty" is defined as discussed above under the Executive exemption, i.e., principal, main, major, or most important duty.

- "Discretion and independent judgment" involves the comparison and the evaluation of possible courses of conduct, and acting or making a decision after the various possibilities have been considered. The term does not require that the decisions made by the employee have a finality that goes with unlimited authority and a complete absence of review.

- "Matters of significance" refers to the level of importance or consequence of the work performed.

The office work or non-manual work of an exempt administrative employee must be directly related to the management policies or general business operations of the employer or the employer's customers. According to the regulations, this phrase describes those types of activities that relate to the administrative operations of a business as distinguished from production operations or sales work. The administrative exemption is limited to persons who participate in formulating management policies, including those whose responsibility it is to carry them out. The regulations also recognize that it is not possible to set down specific rules that will define the precise point at which work becomes of substantial importance to the operation of the business. Suffice it to observe that the work under consideration must not be routine or clerical in nature. For instance, bookkeepers, secretaries, and clerks are routinely not exempt. Such employees are viewed as "production" workers rather than policy makers. Tax experts, credit managers, account executives, brokers, sales research experts, and personnel/human resources directors are typical examples of employees who would be considered as exempt.

In determining whether an employee exercises "discretion and independent judgment with respect to matters of significance," consider whether the employee: has authority to formulate, affect, interpret, or implement management policies or operating practices; carries out major assignments in conducting the operations of the business; performs work that affects business operations to a substantial degree, even if the employee's assignments are related to operations of a particular segment of the business; has authority to commit the employer in matters that have significant financial impact; has authority to waive or deviate from established policies or procedures without prior approval; has authority to negotiate and bind the company on significant matters; provides consultation or expert advice to management; is involved in planning long or short-term business objectives; investigates and resolves matters of significance on behalf of management; and represents the company in handling complaints, arbitrating disputes or resolving grievances.

Employers claiming an administrative exemption must be prepared to argue the position that an employee's primary duties require discretion and independent judgment. The distinction between exempt administrative employees and non-exempt employees whose work is administrative is sometimes articulated as the distinction between those who are engaged in the managing of the business and not merely the day-to-day carrying out of its affairs.

Defining the Professional Exemption

Two types of professional employees are recognized as exempt under the Act: "learned professionals" and "creative professionals."

Professional Exemption

The Learned Professional

To qualify as an exempt learned professional, an employee has to earn a salary of $455 or more weekly and have as his/her "primary duty" the performance of (i) "work requiring knowledge of an advanced type;" (ii) in a "field of science or learning;" and (iii) "customarily acquired by a prolonged course of specialized intellectual instruction."

- "Work requiring knowledge of an advanced type" means work which is predominantly intellectual in character and which includes work requiring the consistent exercise of discretion and judgment.

- "Field of science or learning" means occupations that have a recognized professional status (doctor, lawyer, engineer, chemist, accountant);

- "Customarily acquired by a prolonged course of specialized intellectual instruction" really means the profession requires the job holder to have a particular degree or have completed specialized academic training. While the occasional chemist who does not have a degree in chemistry may fit, cases like that will be the exception and not the rule.

Creative Professionals

To qualify as an exempt creative professional, an employee must meet the $455 or greater weekly salary test and have as his/her primary duty work that requires (i) "invention, imagination, originality or talent;" and (ii) "in a recognized field of artistic or creative endeavor."

- "Invention, imagination, originality or talent" refers to work that requires more than mere intelligence, diligence and accuracy. A cartoonist who is given a concept and develops a cartoon is covered whereas the animator who brings the cartoon to life would not be exempted.

♦ "In a recognized field of artistic or creative endeavor" includes fields such as music, writing and acting and excludes routine mental, manual, mechanical or physical work that someone with general manual or intellectual ability and training could perform.

Teachers

Any employee with a primary duty of teaching, tutoring, instructing or lecturing in the activity of imparting knowledge and who is employed and engaged in this activity as a teacher in an educational establishment by which the employee is employed is a "Professional" and exempt from the overtime and minimum wage requirements of the FLSA.

Teaching consists of lecturing, tutoring, instructing and similar activities for the purpose of imparting knowledge. Personnel engaged in teaching may include regular academic teachers, teachers at the kindergarten or nursery school level, teachers of gifted or disabled children, teachers of skilled or semi-skilled trades and occupations, automobile instructors, aircraft flight instructors, home economics teachers, and vocal or instrumental music teachers. The contribution of a significant amount of a teacher's time to extracurricular activities such as athletic coaching or acting as a drama advisor has no bearing on a teacher's exempt status. The extracurricular activities are simply a recognized part of a school's contribution to the educational development of the student.

Certification by the state or being employed in a school setting is not sufficient to support exempt status, if the individual is not in fact employed and engaged as a teacher. A teacher will be exempt only when his or her "primary duty" is imparting knowledge. Uncertified private school teachers who are not required to secure a teaching certificate may qualify as exempt employees if they can meet all the requirements of the teaching exemption.

Outside Sales Exemption

Outside salespeople are exempt from the overtime and minimum wage requirements of the FLSA. The exemption applies to salespeople in both retail and non-retail operations. There is no minimum compensation that a salesperson must receive to qualify for the exemption. The exemption only covers salespeople who have as their "primary duty" the task of making outside sales or obtaining orders or contracts for services or for the use of facilities for which a consideration will be paid by the client or customer. There is no longer a requirement that 80% of the salesman's time be spent conducting sales away from the employer's place of business in order for that task to be the person's primary duty. Sales activities to which the exemption applies include any sale, exchange, contract to sell, consignment for sale, shipment for sale, and transfer of title to property. "Obtaining orders or contracts...for the use of facilities" includes selling radio and television time, and advertising space in newspapers and periodicals.

This exemption only applies to salespeople who are regularly engaged in conducting such sales activities **away from the employer's place of business**. Thus, selling at any of the employer's offices or facilities does not qualify. Additionally, selling or making telephone solicitations from any other regularly used location, including the salesperson's home, will not be considered outside sales. With the growth of telemarketing and use of email and the internet for sales activities, the amount of time spent away from the employer's place of business for many traditional outside sales employees has declined to the point that reliance on the outside sales exemption is risky.

Driver-Salespeople

The eligibility of driver-salespeople for the outside sales exemption depends on whether they are primarily employed for the purpose of making sales. Many factors are germane to this determination but "yes" answers to the following questions normally will indicate the driver is an exempt outside salesperson if he or she:

- Provides the only sales contact between the employer and the customers visited, calls on customers and takes orders for products, delivers products from stock in the employee's vehicle or procures and delivers the product to the customer on a later trip, and receives compensation commensurate with the volume of products sold;

- Obtains or solicits orders for the employer's products from persons who have authority to commit the customer for purchases;

- Calls on new prospects for customers along the employee's route and attempts to convince them of the desirability of accepting regular delivery of goods; or

- Calls on established customers along the route and persuades regular customers to accept delivery of increased amounts of goods or new products, even though the initial sale or agreement for delivery was made by someone else.

The regulations also state that a driver would not qualify for the outside sales exemption if he or she:

- Is a route driver whose primary duty is to transport products sold by the employer through vending machines and to keep such machines stocked, in good operating condition and in good locations;

- Often calls on established customers every day or every week but cannot try to sell more products to the customer; or the amount of the sale is determined by the volume of the customer's sales since the previous delivery; or

- Primarily engaged in making deliveries to customers and performs activities intended to promote sales by customers (including placing point-of-sale and other advertising materials, price stamping commodities, arranging merchandise on shelves, in coolers or in cabinets, rotating stock according to date; and cleaning and otherwise servicing display cases), unless such work is in furtherance of the driver's own sales efforts.

Sales trainers and helpers who are not directly engaged in making sales are not covered by the outside sales exemption. A driver who does not qualify as an outside sales employee, but who is engaged in interstate driving, may qualify for exemption under the Motor Courier Act as discussed below.

The Computer-Related Occupation Exemption

Under the regulations, the computer-related occupation exemption applies to employees who:

- Meet the $455 or greater weekly salary test or are compensated on an hourly basis at a rate of not less than $27.63/hour; and

- Have as their primary duty:

    - the application of systems analysis techniques and procedures, including consulting with users, to determine hardware, software, or system functional specifications;

    - the design, development, documentation, analysis, creation, testing or modification of computer systems or programs, including prototypes, based on and related to user or system design specifications;

    - the design, documentation, testing, creation, or modification of computer programs related to machine operating systems; or

    - A combination of the aforementioned duties, the performance of which requires the same level of skills.

Commonly used job titles which may be encompassed by this exemption include computer programmer, systems analyst, computer systems analyst, computer programmer analyst, applications programmer, applications systems analyst, applications systems analyst/programmer, software engineer, software specialist, systems engineer, and systems specialist. However, this list is not all inclusive, nor are job titles alone determinative of exempt status.

The exemption does not apply to those employees who manufacture, repair, or maintain computer hardware or to people who use computers e.g., CAD/CAM operators. Unlike the exemption for learned professionals, the exemption for computer occupations is not delineated in terms of the process by which the high degree of skill is acquired, such as an academic degree.

The regulations anticipate that an employee will normally gain the expertise and skill required to qualify for this exemption through a combination of education and job experience. Because this exemption is meant to apply only to those sophisticated employees who have gained a high level of proficiency and expertise, trainees and employees in entry-level positions will seldom qualify for exempt status.

Exemption for Highly Compensated Workers

A new exemption has been created for individuals who earn $100,000 or more annually (and also earn at least $455 on a weekly basis) and who (i) perform office or non-manual work as their primary duty, and (ii) who customarily and regularly perform at lest one of the exempt duties or responsibilities of an executive, administrative, or professional employee. The regulations discuss what payments are includable in salary, and how to prorate annual compensation for those who work for less than a year. The regulations allow an employer to make at the end of a year additional payments to employees to satisfy the salary requirement.

The Salary Basis Requirement

Even under those circumstances which demonstrate that an employee meets the primary duty test for exemption, it is still possible that the exempt status can be lost or forfeited if the employee is not paid on a true salary basis. This loss of exempt status may occur when an employer imposes impermissible deductions from an exempt employee's salary. To meet the "salary basis" requirement, an employee must be paid a predetermined amount which is not subject to reduction regardless of the quality or quantity of work. Further, the exempt employee must receive his full salary for any week that he performs work without regard to the number of hours worked. Thus, an exempt employee's salary may only be subject to deductions in certain situations.

Permissible and
Non-Permissible Deductions

Deductions may be taken when the employee has performed no work in a week, or where the employee is absent for a full day for personal reasons other than illness or an accident. Deductions may also be made for absences of one or more full days where the deduction is made in accordance with a bona fide plan, policy or practice of providing compensation for loss of salary due to sickness, where the employee has not yet become eligible to participate in the plan or has exhausted all accrued leave there under. Where an employee has violated a major safety rule, an employer may impose a deduction from the employee's salary. Likewise, deductions for full day suspensions of less than a full week can be imposed for "serious workplace misconduct" if there is a written and published policy that specifies that all employees are subject to suspension for violation of the rule(s) in question, e.g., rules prohibiting sexual harassment, violence, drug or alcohol violations, and violations of state or federal laws.

Generally, deductions from pay may not be made for partial days of absence for any reason. The Department of Labor enforcement policy permits partial day deductions against accrued sick days or personal days, but NOT against actual pay received. If an exempt employee works any part of the work day, the employee must receive full pay for that day under the salary basis test. However, partial pay deductions may be made for leave taken under the Family Medical Leave Act without jeopardizing the FLSA exemption, if such absence constitutes intermittent or reduced leave under the FMLA.

Improper Deductions

An otherwise exempt employee may lose exempt status where the employer improperly imposes deductions from their salary. Thus, an exempt managerial employee may be transformed into a non-exempt employee. The loss of the exemption may continue for the period during which the policy authorizing these impermissible deductions was in effect.

An employer that makes an isolated inadvertent and impermissible deduction from an exempt employee's salary, e.g. the employer makes deductions for partial days of absence due to personal reasons, can salvage the exempt status classification of that employee if the employer devises and disseminates a written policy that prohibits improper pay deductions and alerts employees to their right to have deductions from their pay reviewed and corrected. The procedure the employee is to follow to make a complaint should be clearly described in that policy and retaliation for using the policy prohibited. The reimbursement mechanism should also be described.

Overtime or Other Additional Pay for Salaried Employees

It is permissible to pay exempt employees additional amounts for work over an above the normal schedule, and such payments may be made on an hourly rate equivalent to the employee's normal earnings without defeating the salary basis requirement. However, if an employer pays overtime on an hourly basis; makes deductions from sick/personal days on an hourly basis; and creates a "debit" against accumulation of future sick/personal days when an employee misses work after sick/personal days are used up; then the employee is compensated in every material respect on an hourly basis and there is a risk that the employer's policy will be considered the equivalent of an hourly rate, and that the salary basis requirement will not be met.

Motor Carrier Act Exemption

Certain employees in transportation-related jobs are exempt from the overtime (but not minimum wage) provisions of the FLSA. The purpose of this exemption is to avoid a conflict with the authority of the U.S. Secretary of Transportation. Under the Motor Carrier Act, the Secretary of Transportation is empowered to regulate motor carriers engaged in interstate commerce. This includes the power to establish qualifications and maximum hours of service for employees of such carriers.

As a general rule, employees are subject to the jurisdiction of the Secretary of Transportation (and exempt from the FLSA overtime provisions) if they drive across state lines carrying property for an employer engaged in interstate commerce. The percentage of an employee's time which is spent transporting goods or passengers across state lines need not be large. Generally, under Department of Labor enforcement policy, employee drivers are considered exempt under the Motor Carrier Act exemption for at least a four month period from the date they engage in interstate transportation, which means that only one trip in a four month period is considered sufficient to activate the exemption.

The Motor Carrier Act overtime exemption is not limited to drivers. Other employees whose activities directly affect the safety of operations of motor vehicles used in interstate commerce also qualify for the exemption. In addition to drivers, the Secretary of Transportation has determined that three other categories of workers perform activities affecting the safe operation of such vehicles. These are drivers' helpers, loaders and mechanics. Only those four types of employees are covered by the Motor Carrier Act exemption from overtime pay.

Commissioned Salespeople

Normally, commissions paid to employees must be counted as part of their compensation for calculating their regular hourly rate and overtime pay. However, employees of retail and service establishments who are paid commissions may be exempt from the overtime requirements of the FLSA under §7(i).

In order to qualify for the exemption, the pay received by the retail or service establishment employee must meet two requirements:

- The employee's regular rate of pay for every hour worked must be more than one and one-half times the minimum wage rate; and

- More than half of the employee's compensation for a representative period, not less than one month, must consist of commissions on goods and services.

For this commission salesperson exemption to apply, the employer must be a "retail or service establishment," which requires that the business:

- Receive at least 75 percent of its annual dollar volume from sales of goods, services or both, which (a) are not for resale; and (b) are recognized as retail sales or services in the particular industry; and

♦ Receive at least 50 percent of its annual dollar volume from sales within the state in which the establishment is located.

In addition, the Supreme Court has interpreted the definition of "retail or service establishment" very restrictively. The Court has indicated that only retailers of goods or services frequently acquired for personal or family use fall within the exemption. Examples of such qualifying businesses which were cited by the Court include hardware stores, clothing stores, shoe stores and furniture stores, as well as automobile dealers (of passenger vehicles), drug stores and department stores.

For the purpose of determining what portion of a commission salesperson's compensation is derived from commissions, different types of commission plans are permissible. The FLSA simply requires that a "bona fide commission rate" be used. Thus, commissions may be based on a percentage of total sales, sales in excess of certain amounts or some other formula. In determining whether commissions received by a salesperson are sufficient to fall within the exemption, it does not matter whether the commissions exceed the salesperson's draw or guarantee.

Seasonal Amusement and Recreation Establishments

Establishments which are amusement or recreational operations, and which are seasonal, are exempt from the minimum wage and overtime provisions of the FLSA. In order to be considered "seasonal," the establishment must meet two tests:

♦ It must not operate more than seven months in any calendar year; and

♦ During the preceding calendar year, its average receipts for any 6 months of the year must not have been more than 33 1/3 percent of its average receipts for the other 6 months of the year.

To qualify as an "amusement or recreational" establishment, it must be one which is frequented by the public for amusement or recreational purposes. Examples include concessionaries at amusement parks and beaches. A private country club open only part of the year may qualify for the exemption regardless of the fact that it is not open to the public.

In 1977, Congress amended this exemption to include organized camps, as well as religious or nonprofit educational conference centers, which meet the seasonality tests. The same amendments disallowed the exemption for private employers operating concessions in national parks, national forests or within the National Wildlife Refuge System.

How to Determine Whether an Exemption Applies

The primary duty test for each of the White Collar exemptions is highly subjective. There is no "bright line" test or any other fool-proof method to determine whether an exemption is available for any particular job category, nor is there any government approved list of jobs approved for exempt status. Job duties, not job title, determine whether a position will be treated as exempt. Accordingly, analyzing detailed job descriptions against the exemption criteria to determine whether the position qualifies as exempt is a reliable methodology only to the extent that the job description is accurate. Therefore, it is essential that the Employer interview the employees who perform the job to be analyzed about their actual day-to-day work duties and modify the written description to mirror the reality.

The information collected from the employee must be specific, detailed and factual – not just a brief collection of conclusory statements. The employee must be given adequate time to prepare the response and should not be "led" into providing evidence to support any particular conclusion. Information provided by the employee should be reviewed and verified by the employee's supervisor.

An example of a Questionnaire that could be used to collect information from employees is provided.

SAMPLE QUESTIONNAIRE FOR DETERMINATION OF EXEMPT STATUS FOR THE WHITE COLLAR EXEMPTIONS

[This sample questionnaire is intended only as a starting point for developing a questionnaire tailored to the particular business of the employer, and to the categories of employees being studied. The results of this questionnaire cannot be taken as resolving the question of exempt status, but may be useful in the employer's determination of that question, and as evidence in the event the question comes up later in an audit or lawsuit.]

GENERAL JOB SUMMARY

What is the primary duty/major purpose or most important duty of your job?

_____
_____
_____
_____
_____
_____
_____

NATURE OF WORK

Do you regularly perform manual work? Yes_____ No_____ If yes, please describe the manual work you perform and estimate the percentage of your time during the year spent performing manual work?

_____
_____
_____
_____
_____
_____
_____

If the answer to the prior question above is "no," does your work primarily consist of office or non-manual work? Please explain what types of office/non-manual work you perform.

_____
_____
_____
_____
_____
_____
_____

MAJOR JOB DUTIES

List each of the major duties performed in the normal course of your job. Indicate the average percentage of time spent each week performing each separate duty. Try to summarize and combine duties so that each statement describes activities that take at least 10% of your overall time. After all the duties have been listed, rank them in the order of importance with #1 being the most important.

If the weekly breakdown varies over the course of the year, please describe how it varies and the number of weeks involved in the fourth column.

Normal number of hours worked per week: _____

Rank Order	% of Hours Per Week	Description of Major Duties/Responsibilities	Describe variations during the year

COMPLEXITY AND SCOPE OF WORK PERFORMED

Is your work primarily involved with administration; which means performing administrative work directly related to the management policies or general business operations of the company or its customers (e.g. formulating policy, advising and making recommendations to management, planning, negotiating, representing the company, purchasing or conducting research? Please explain.

_____
_____
_____
_____
_____

Describe what makes your work routine complicated, unusual or difficult to perform. What obstacles are there in the work itself that makes it difficult to accomplish?

_____
_____
_____
_____
_____

Do your duties involve advising superiors, planning, negotiating, or representing your department in matters affecting Company policies or procedures? Describe.

_____
_____
_____
_____
_____

Do you formulate policy? Describe.

_____
_____
_____
_____

Is your work of substantial importance to the overall management or operation of your area or department? Explain.

_____
_____
_____
_____
_____

Are there other employees doing the same sort of work or carrying out assignments of the same relative importance? If so, please describe.

_____
_____
_____
_____
_____

SUPERVISORY CONTROLS

List which of the tasks from the "major duties" section (by the "rank" number) that you do without necessarily receiving new instructions each time from your supervisor.

_____
_____
_____
_____

What is the nature of any standing or continuing instructions you have been given regarding these tasks (check one)

_____ Instructions are detailed, specific and cover all aspects of the work

_____ Instructions are somewhat general; many aspects of the work are covered specifically, but I must also use some judgment

_____ Instructions are very general; I must use much judgment

_____ Other (describe fully). _____
_____

What is the nature of the instructions your supervisor gives you when assigning new or one-time tasks? (Check one)

_____ Detailed, specific and cover all aspects of the work

_____ Somewhat general, covering many aspects of the work

_____ Direction provided in terms of broadly defined missions or functions

_____ Other (describe fully)

How does your supervisor (or another employee) review your work? (Check all that apply?

_____ My supervisor spot-checks what I am doing as I do it.

_____ My supervisor spot-checks my competed work

_____ My supervisor reviews most or all of my work while am doing it

_____ My supervisor reviews most or all of my completed work

_____ My supervisor does not review my work

_____ Other (describe fully)

DISCRETION AND INDEPENDENT JUDGMENT

If possible, list three decisions you are required to make independently, using your own judgment and discretion as to how to decide.

_____

_____

_____

_____

_____

List three decisions about which you are required to seek consultation with, or approval from, a superior.

_____

_____

_____

GUIDELINES

What written guidelines or procedures do you use in your work? (How do you know, other than from what your supervisor tells you, what tasks you are to perform and how they are to be accomplished?)

_____

_____

_____

_____

_____

Do the guidelines you use in your work require interpretation or are they clear and specific?

_____
_____
_____
_____
_____

Do you ever have to determine which guideline to apply in a specific situation? If so, when? Please give an example.

_____
_____
_____
_____
_____

SUPERVISORY RESPONSIBILITIES

If you manage a recognized group, unit, department or subdivision of the Company, identify that group, unit, department or subdivision. For purposes of this question, "management" includes, but is not limited to, activities such as:

- interviewing, selecting and training employees;

- setting and adjusting or effectively recommending rates of pay and hours of work of employees;

- scheduling and directing the work of other employees;

- evaluating the work of other employees for the purpose of recommending or effectively recommending promotions or other changes in status;

- disciplining or effectively recommending discipline for employees;

- handling employee complaints and grievances;

- planning the work of other employees ad apportioning work among employees;

- determining the type of materials, supplies and equipment to be used by employees and controlling the distribution of material and supplies to employees; and

- providing for the safety of employees.

How many full-time employees (or full-time equivalents) do you supervise?

_____
_____
_____
_____
_____

If you perform any of the management duties described above, list each such duty you perform and estimate the percentage of time you spend in the workweek performing each duty:

% of Work	Description of management duty

Do you spend part of the workweek performing the same type of work as that being performed by the employees you supervise? If so, describe that work and estimate the percentage of time in the workweek you spend performing that work:

% of Work	Description of duties

Describe the kind of supervision you exercise over those listed above.

_____

_____

_____

_____

_____

What percentage of your time overall is spent supervising this group: _____%

What percentage of your time is spent performing the same work as other members of the group? _____%

PROFESSIONAL QUALIFICATIONS

Does your work required a specialized degree, or the equivalent in education and experience (as opposed to a general academic education)? In what field?

_____
_____
_____
_____
_____

What specialized degree, or the equivalent in education and experience, do you possess?

_____
_____
_____
_____
_____

If you perform duties that require a specialized course of education, describe those duties and the percentage of time in the workweek you send performing those duties.

% of Work	Description of duties

SALES WORK

Do you perform sales activities from a fixed site? If so, where? Whayt percentage of your workweek is spent performing sales activities from a fixed site?

_____
_____
_____
_____

Do you perform outside sales activities (i.e. conducting sales activities at your customers' residence or place of business)? If so, what percentage of your workweek is spent performing outside sales activities (including travel to and from your customers' places of business?

_____
_____
_____
_____

If you perform outside sales activities, what percentage of your workweek is spent performing tasks directly related to your outside sales activities (e.g. preparing sales reports and documentation, planning your travel itinerary and assembling or organizing sales manuals for customers)?

_____
_____
_____
_____
_____
_____

COMPUTER-RELATED WORK

Does your work involve the application of systems analysis techniques and procedures, including consulting with users, to determine hardware, software, or system functional specifications? If so, please describe the work you do that fits this description and estimate the percentage of time in the workweek you spend performing this type of work.

% of Work	Description of duties

Does your work involve the design, development, documentation, analysis, creation, testing, or modification of computer systems or programs based on and related to user or system design specifications? If so, please describe the work you do that fits this description and estimate the percentage of time in the workweek you spend performing this type of work.

% of Work	Description of duties

Does your work involve the design, documentation, testing, creation or modification of computer programs related to the operation of machinery? If so, please describe the work you do that fits this description and estimate the percentage of time in the workweek you spend performing this type of work.

% of Workweek	Description of work

Does your work involve the repair, installation or maintenance of computer software, hardware and related equipment? If so, please describe the work you do that fits this description and estimate the percentage of time in the workweek you spend performing this type of work.

% of Workweek	Description of work

Does your work involve training others about how to use hardware or software, answering their questions about the use of hardware or software, or responding to requests for help regarding problems with hardware or software? If so, please describe the work you do that fits this description and estimate the percentage of time in the workweek you spend performing this type of work.

% of Workweek	Description of work

ADDITIONAL INFORMATION

(Attach additional sheets if needed)

Example. Very low interest rates over the last few years have resulted in a boom in real estate sales, home financing and refinancing. This has resulted in a big increase in the employment of loan originators (LOs) employed by finance companies. Typical LOs use leads to make phone contact with potential customers. Following standard operating procedures and company guidelines, the LOs try to match a customer's needs with various loan products, obtain the information needed to complete a loan application, run credit reports and then move the application to a loan underwriter who decides whether to approve the loan. If approved, the LO prepares the papers for closing. LOs generally negotiate the number of points to be paid by the customer within a predetermined floor/ceiling. A typical LO is paid a salary plus commissions. Many companies who employ LOs have treated them as exempt. Thus, they do not track the hours worked by LOs, do not pay LOs overtime for hours over 40 and do not treat the commission earnings of the LOs as part of the LOs regular rate. After all, these employers have reasoned, how could someone earning $65,000 – 100,000 or more (as many LOs do) NOT be exempt?

Unfortunately, earning lots of money does not automatically qualify an employee as exempt. Because LOs do not supervise other employees, they do not qualify as executives. They are performing the employer's basic production work; not work related to their employer's "general business operations," nor does their work require discretion and independent judgment. Thus, they do not qualify under the administrative exemption. The work does not require a professional degree, so that exemption is not available. LOs are not covered by the §7(i) exemption for commission paid retail or service establishment employees, since this is not considered a "retail" business for this purpose. Nor are LOs covered by the outside sales exemption since the work of an LO is almost always performed from phones and computers located in the employer's office. Hence, it should come as no surprise that beginning in 2001 a rash of lawsuits successfully vindicating the right of LOs to overtime were filed and continue to be filed. Substantial overtime back pay awards have been granted.

Other job categories often questionably treated as exempt include:

- loan officers
- inside sales employees
- account executives
- insurance agents
- insurance appraisers
- escrow/mortgage closers
- customer service representatives
- bookkeepers
- paralegals and legal assistants
- buyers
- executive secretaries
- administrative/executive assistants
- technicians
- inspectors
- assistant managers

Employees with these titles may, in fact, qualify for an exemption if the specific duties performed satisfy the primary duty test and if the salary basis test is also satisfied, but in each case noted above, courts have found employees with the same or equivalent titles non-exempt based on the facts presented in that particular situation.

The Computer Occupation Professional

Under the regulations, the computer professional exemption applies to employees who are highly skilled in computer systems analysis, programming or related work in software functions. Job titles which may be encompassed by this exemption include:

- computer programmer
- systems analyst
- computer systems analyst
- computer programmer analyst
- applications programmer
- applications systems analyst
- applications systems analyst/programmer
- software engineer
- software specialist
- systems engineer
- systems specialist

However, this list is not all inclusive, nor are job titles alone determinative of exempt status. Payment on a salary basis is not required so long as the other requirements for the computer professional exemption are met and the computer professional's hourly rate of pay exceeds $27.63 an hour.

Also, under the regulations, the exemption does not apply to those employees who manufacture, repair or maintain computer hardware. Unlike the exemption for learned professionals, the exemption for computer occupations is not delineated in terms of the process by which the high degree of skill is acquired, such as an academic degree. The regulations anticipate that an employee will normally gain the expertise and skill required to qualify for this exemption through a combination of education and job experience. Because this exemption is meant to apply only to those sophisticated employees who have gained a high level of proficiency and expertise, trainees and employees in entry-level positions will seldom qualify for exempt status.

Under the applicable regulations, work that involves "theoretical and practical application of highly-specialized knowledge in computer systems analysis, programming and software engineering" meets the duties test of the special exemption for computer professionals. The regulations illustrate the types of computer-related professions that qualify for the exemption. Specifically, for a computer professional to be exempt from the overtime requirement, his other primary duties must include:

- the application of systems analysis techniques and procedures, including consulting with users to determine hardware, software or system specifications;

- the design, development, documentation, analysis, creation, testing or modification of computer systems or programs, including prototypes, based on and related to user or system design specifications;

- the design, documentation, testing, creation or modification of computer systems or programs related to machine operating systems; or

- a combination of the above-described duties that requires the same level of skill.

The regulations for this category provide an objective set of criteria; however, using a questionnaire to gather information about actual job duties is also helpful.

SAMPLE QUESTIONNAIRE FOR DETERMINATION OF EXEMPT STATUS FOR COMPUTER RELATED OCCUPATIONS UNDER PUBLIC LAW 101-583

[This sample questionnaire is intended only as a starting point for developing a Questionnaire tailored to the particular business of the employer, and to the categories of employees being studied. The results of this questionnaire cannot be taken as resolving the question of exempt status, but may be useful in the employer's determination of that question, and as evidence in the event the question comes up later in an audit or lawsuit. This questionnaire does not address qualification for exemption as executive, administrative or professional employees.]

1. Does the employee work independently and generally without close supervision?

2. Has the employee achieved a level of proficiency in the theoretical and practical application of a body of highly-specialized knowledge in computer systems analysis, programming and software engineering?

3. Does the employee's "primary duty," (*i.e.*, more than half the employee's time) fall into one of the categories described below?

    • Application of systems analysis techniques and procedures, including consulting with users, to determine hardware, software or system functional specifications; or

    • Design, development, documentation, analysis, creation, testing or modification of computer systems or programs, including prototypes, based on and related to user or system design specifications; or

    • Design, documentation, testing, creation or modification of computer programs related to machine operating systems; or

    • A combination of the aforementioned duties, the performance of which requires the same level of skills.

4. Is the employee paid at a rate equivalent to $27.63 per hour?

THIS DOCUMENT HAS BEEN PREPARED BY ICE MILLER ONLY TO SERVE AS A GUIDE IN DEVELOPING AN APPROPRIATE POLICY OR AGREEMENT. AN EMPLOYER SHOULD CONSULT WITH COUNSEL CONCERNING HOW THIS GUIDE SHOULD BE USED IN LIGHT OF ANY PARTICULAR FACTUAL SITUATION, AND TO DISCUSS CHANGES WHICH MAY HAVE OCCURRED IN THE UNDERLYING LAW AND REGULATIONS.

The Salary Basis Requirement

Even under those circumstances which demonstrate an employee is exempt from overtime compensation under the FLSA, it is still possible that the exempt status can be lost or forfeited if the employee is not paid on a true salary basis. This loss of exempt status may occur when an employer imposes impermissible deductions from an exempt employee's salary. To meet the "salary basis" requirement, an employee must be paid a predetermined amount which is not subject to reduction regardless of the quality or quantity of work. Further, the exempt employee must receive his or her full salary for any week that he performs work without regard to the number of hours worked. Thus, an exempt employee's salary may only be subject to deductions in certain situations.

Permissible and Non-Permissible Deductions

Deductions may be taken when the employee has performed no work in a week, or where the employee is absent for a full day for personal reasons other than illness or an accident. Deductions may also be made for absences of one or more full days, if the deduction is made in accordance with a bona fide plan, policy or practice of providing compensation for loss of salary due to sickness, and the employee has not yet become eligible to participate in the plan or has exhausted all accrued leave thereunder. If an employee has violated a major safety rule, an employer may impose a deduction from the employee's salary, but this is the ONLY deduction permitted for disciplinary reason.

Generally, deductions from pay may not be made for partial days of absence for any reason. The Department of Labor enforcement policy permits partial day deductions against accrued sick days or personal days, but NOT against actual pay received. If an exempt employee works any part of the work day, the employee must receive full pay for that day under the salary basis test. However, partial pay deductions may be made for leave taken under the Family and Medical Leave Act without jeopardizing the FLSA exemption, if such absence constitutes intermittent or reduced leave under the FMLA.

Disciplinary Deductions

A word of caution is in order here. An otherwise exempt employee may lose exempt status if the employer imposes deductions from his or her salary for disciplinary purposes. Thus, an exempt managerial employee may be transformed into a non-exempt employee. An actual finding of a disciplinary deduction need not be established if there is a showing that the disciplinary policy creates a "significant likelihood" that the deduction may be made. The loss of the exemption may continue for the period during which the policy authorizing these impermissible deductions was in effect.

Window of Correction

In the event an employer makes an inadvertent and impermissible deduction from an exempt employee's salary, *e.g.* the employer makes deductions for partial days of absence due to personal reasons, it is still possible to salvage the exempt status classification of that employee. The "salary basis" regulations provide that "[w]here a deduction not permitted by these interpretations is inadvertent, or is made for reasons other than lack of work, the exemption will not be considered to have been lost if the employer reimburses the employee for such deductions and promises to comply in the future." This window of correction is not available where the deductions were made because there is no work available or hours are shortened due to a business slowdown. The DOL reasons that deductions made due to a business slowdown indicates that there is no intention to pay the employee on a salary basis.

Overtime or Other Additional Pay for Salaried Employees

It is permissible to pay exempt employees additional amounts for work over and above the normal schedule, and such payments may be made on an hourly rate equivalent to the employee's normal earnings without defeating the salary basis requirement. However, if an employer pays overtime on an hourly basis; makes deductions from sick/personal days on an hourly basis; and creates a "debit" against accumulation of future sick/personal days when an employee misses work after sick/personal days are used up, then the employee is compensated in every material respect on an hourly basis. At least one court has held that such a de facto hourly rate does defeat the salary basis requirement, with literally no situation in which an employee's pay is fixed even though the amount of work performed varies.

Outside Sales Exemption

Outside salespeople are exempt from the overtime and minimum wage requirements of the FLSA. The exemption applies to salespeople in both retail and non-retail operations. There is no minimum compensation that a salesperson must receive to qualify for the exemption. The exemption only covers outside salespeople who are customarily and regularly engaged in qualifying activities. Those activities must be either:

- selling goods or services; or
- obtaining orders or contracts for services or for the use of facilities.

Sales activities to which the exemption applies include any sale, exchange, contract to sell, consignment for sale, shipment for sale and transfer of title to property. "Obtaining orders or contracts...for the use of facilities" includes selling radio and television time, and advertising space in newspapers and periodicals.

However, this exemption only applies to salespeople who customarily and regularly conduct such sales activities **away from the employer's place of business**. Thus, selling at any of the employer's offices or facilities does not qualify. Additionally, selling or making telephone solicitations from any other regularly used location, including the salesperson's home, will not be considered outside sales. With the growth of telemarketing and use of e-mail and the Internet for sales activities, the amount of time spent away from the employer's place of business for many traditional outside sales employees has declined to the point that reliance on the outside sales exemption is risky.

There is no "primary duty" test for the outside exemption such as exists for the executive, administrative and professional exemptions. However, for the outside sales exemption to apply, the time which the salesperson devotes to activities other than outside selling and outside solicitation of orders cannot exceed 20 percent of the hours worked in a workweek by nonexempt employees of the employer. This 20-percent limit is based on the hours worked by nonexempt employees performing the same kind of nonexempt work that the outside salesperson is performing. If there are no nonexempt employees performing the nonexempt work performed by the outside salesperson, the 20-percent limit applies to a 40 hour workweek. In that case, the outside salesperson could spend no more than 8 hours per week performing nonexempt work without losing the exemption.

Excluded from the 20-percent limit on nonexempt work are activities incidental to and in conjunction with the employee's own outside sales or solicitation. Examples of such "incidental" activities are clerical duties, deliveries, collections, travel and attending sales conferences.

Individuals who both sell and perform the same service are not considered salespeople and, therefore, are not eligible for the outside sales exemption. The reason: selling the service is incidental to performing it, and service work is nonexempt (unless it qualifies for some other exemption, such as the professional exemption).

Example: Marty, the top sales person for Acme Products, used to spend four days on the road calling on customers, and the fifth day back at the office completing paperwork for sales made. He was clearly qualified for the outside sales exemption. However, several of Acme's major customers now purchase online through the Acme website, and Marty is able to complete these sales using e-mail and the telephone/fax for follow-up. Marty is still on the road three or four days a month and has increased his sales volume, even though he spends much more time in the office.

Due to the changes in technology and sales practices, Marty no longer qualifies, even though he is selling to the same customers in increased volumes and is making substantially more money as a commissioned sales employee. Acme could be liable to Marty for substantial overtime pay, even though he is already one of the company's highest paid employees. A properly drafted agreement based on the fixed salary (including commissions) agreement for fluctuating hours would limit that to additional half-time for hours worked over 40.

Driver-Salespeople

The eligibility of driver-salespeople for the outside sales exemption depends on whether they are primarily employed for the purpose of making sales. Many factors are germane to this determination but "yes" answers to the following questions normally will indicate the driver is an exempt outside salesperson:

- Is the driver being paid primarily on the basis of volume of sales attributable to the driver's own effort?

- Does the driver serve as the only sales contact between the employer and the customers to whom the driver delivers?

- Does the driver take orders for products the driver delivers?

- Does the driver persuade regular customers to increase the amounts of products the driver delivers?

- Does the driver contact prospective new customers for purchases?

Sales trainers and helpers who are not directly engaged in making sales are not covered by the outside sales exemption.

Motor Carrier Act Exemption

Certain employees in transportation-related jobs are exempt from the overtime (but not minimum wage) provisions of the FLSA. The purpose of this exemption is to avoid a conflict with the authority of the U.S. Secretary of Transportation. Under the Motor Carrier Act, the Secretary of Transportation is empowered to regulate motor carriers engaged in interstate commerce. This includes the power to establish qualifications and maximum hours of service for employees of such carriers. As a general rule, employees are subject to the jurisdiction of the Secretary of Transportation (and exemption from the FLSA overtime provision) if they drive across state lines carrying property for an employer engaged in interstate commerce. However, the percentage of an employee's time which is spent transporting goods or passengers across state lines need not be large. Generally, under Department of Labor enforcement policy, employee drivers are considered exempt under the Motor Carrier Act exemption for at least a four-month period from the date they engage in interstate transportation, which means that only one trip in a four-month period is considered sufficient to activate the exemption. Even drivers who transport goods solely within a state may be exempt if they receive from or deliver to other drivers' goods or passengers those other drivers have transported or will transport across one or more state lines; however, the facts and circumstances of such intrastate continuation of interstate commerce should be carefully reviewed before relying on the exemption.

The Motor Carrier Act overtime exemption is not limited to drivers. Other employees whose activities directly affect the safety of operations of motor vehicles used in interstate commerce also qualify for the exemption. In addition to drivers, the Secretary of Transportation has determined that three other categories of workers perform activities affecting the safe operation of such vehicles. These are drivers' helpers, loaders and mechanics. Only those four types of employees are covered by the Motor Carrier Act exemption from overtime pay.

Commissioned Salespeople

Normally, commissions paid to employees must be counted as part of their compensation for calculating their regular hourly rate and overtime pay. However, employees of retail and service establishments who are paid commissions may be exempt from the overtime requirements of the FLSA under §7(i).

In order to qualify for the exemption, the pay received by the retail or service establishment must meet two requirements:

- The employee's regular rate of pay must be more than one and one-half times the minimum wage rate.

- More than half of the employee's compensation for a representative period, not less than one month, must consist of commissions on goods and services.

For this commission salesperson exemption to apply, the employer must be a "retail or service establishment," which requires that the business:

- receive at least 75 percent of its annual dollar volume from sales of goods, services or both, which (a) are not for resale; and (b) are recognized as retail sales or services in the particular industry; and

- receive at least 50 percent of its annual dollar volume from sales within the state in which the establishment is located.

In addition, the Supreme Court has interpreted the definition of "retail or service establishment" very restrictively. The Court has indicated that only retailers of goods or services frequently acquired for personal or family use fall within the exemption. Examples of such qualifying businesses cited by the Court include hardware stores, clothing stores, shoe stores and furniture stores, as well as automobile dealers (of passenger vehicles), drug stores and department stores.

For the purpose of determining what portion of a commission salesperson's compensation is derived from commissions, different types of commission plans are permissible. The FLSA simply requires that a "bona fide commission rate" be used. Thus, commissions may be based on a percentage of total sales, sales in excess of certain amounts or some other formula. In determining whether commissions received by a salesperson are sufficient to fall within the exemption, it does not matter whether the commissions exceed the salesperson's draw or guarantee.

Seasonal Amusements and Recreation Establishments

Establishments which are amusement or recreational operations, and which are seasonal, are exempt from the minimum wage and overtime provisions of the FLSA. In order to be considered "seasonal," the establishment must meet two tests:

* it must not operate more than seven months in any calendar year; and

* during the preceding calendar year, its average receipts for any six months of the year must not have been more than 33 1/3 percent of its average receipts for the other six months of the year.

To qualify as an "amusement or recreational" establishment, it must be one which is frequented by the public for amusement or recreational purposes. Examples include concessionaires at amusement parks and beaches. A private country club open only part of the year may qualify for the exemption regardless of the fact that it is not open to the public.

In 1977, Congress amended this exemption to include organized camps, as well as religious or nonprofit educational conference centers, which meet the seasonality tests. The same amendments disallowed the exemption for private employers operating concessions in national parks, national forests or within the National Wildlife Refuge System.

Proposed Regulations to Change Exemption Qualifications

Regulations that dramatically change the white collar exemptions were proposed by the Department of Labor in March 2003. These regulations encountered stiff opposition from labor organizations and other groups, and final approval of the regulations had not occurred as of March 2004. Even if they are promulgated, opponents have threatened congressional action to block implementation of the new regulations.

If these regulations are ultimately approved, they will raise the minimum salary basis requirement to $425 per week, from the current level of $250. An entirely new exemption would be created for employees who earn at least $65,000 per year in total non-discretionary compensation and who have a primary duty of performing office or non-manual work and perform any one of the exempt duties of an executive, administrative or professional employee. The proposed regulations would also replace the ambiguous "discretion in independent judgment" standard for the administrative exemption by requiring that the employee hold a "position of responsibility with the employer," which means performing either "work of substantial importance" or "work requiring a high level of skill or training." The proposed regulations would also eliminate the "discretion of judgment" requirement for professional employees.

Further refinements are included in the proposed regulations for the white collar and outside sales exemptions, and changes in the salary basis requirement are proposed that would permit disciplinary suspensions for a wider variety of violations and would expand the use of the "window of correction" for improper deductions from salaries, among other changes.

Because the proposed regulations have not been adopted (and may never be adopted in anything like their present form) a description of any new regulations will be provided in a supplement to or new edition of this handbook, if and when they are officially promulgated.

.

Chapter 4

Compensable Working Time

This chapter pertains to individuals who are covered by the FLSA and for whom there is no exemption from either minimum wage or overtime requirements, *i.e.* **non-exempt** employees. To comply with the FLSA, an employer must accurately determine and record compensable working time, *i.e.*, activities performed by an employee that require payment. Generally, employers must compensate employees for all work they perform – this seems obvious, but is it? Is a mechanic who reports five minutes before the start of his shift to pick up his tools entitled to compensation? Is a secretary who is permitted a half-hour lunch break entitled to compensation if she answers her telephone? Is an employee who travels a mile across town to a different location during the day entitled to payment? Those and related questions will be answered in this section.

"Suffer or Permit" to Work

The phrase "suffer or permit" to work is a term of art in wage and hour law. "Suffer or permit" refers to time when a non-exempt employee is permitted to work during non-working hours. Many employers believe that issuing a policy prohibiting employees from working during unpaid periods (*e.g.*, lunch hours and before or after their shift) is sufficient to avoid liability. This is incorrect. Management may not rely solely upon a stated policy to avoid liability. If management knows or reasonably should have known that an employee is performing work during non-working hours, the employer must compensate the employee. In addition to promulgating a policy, employers need to take further action to ensure employees are not working during unpaid periods. An exception exists if the work is de minimus (*i.e.*, insubstantial or inconsequential). Compensation is not required for de minimus work.

Example 1: ABC Company is located in rural Indiana. There are no convenience stores or fast food restaurants located nearby. A non-exempt secretary eats lunch at her desk because she prefers it to the lunchroom. Her telephone routinely rings during her unpaid lunch hour. She always answers the telephone and otherwise performs her job while eating at her desk. Is she entitled to compensation? Answer: Yes. The employee is performing her work and the employer is permitting it; therefore, she is entitled to compensation for the time worked. Since this is a routine occurrence, the de minimus exception does not apply.

Example 2: A non-exempt employee worries about finishing a project. His supervisor denied his request to work overtime. Nevertheless, unbeknownst to the supervisor, the employee covertly took the assignment home and completed it. Is the employee entitled to compensation? Answer: No. The employee performed the work without management's knowledge and against management's express denial of overtime; therefore, the time is not compensable. If the supervisor had told the non-exempt employee he could work late as long as he knew he would not be compensated, the employee would be entitled to compensation because the employer "suffered or permitted" the work to occur.

Pre-Shift and Post-Shift Activities

Employees are entitled to compensation for performing "principal activities" even if the activities occur before or after regular work hours. An employee who, at the beginning of her workday, oils, greases and cleans her machine is engaged in a principal work activity integral to the operation. A garment worker who arrives 30 minutes early every day to deliver cloth to each workstation and turn on machines is engaging in a principle work activity. An employee who arrives at work and must change into protective clothing because he works around chemicals is engaged in a principle work activity. In each of these examples, the Department of Labor takes the position that the employees are entitled to compensation for pre- and post-shift activities because they are integral parts of the operation.

Example: Suppose an employer offers shower rooms for employees. Employees are not required to wear uniforms and the work does not involve any toxic materials. Some employees shower after work because they are sweaty and dirty. Is the employer required to compensate employees who take showers? Answer: No. The employer is not required to compensate employees for "shower time" because it is not an integral activity. It is important to note that the answer depends upon the employer's operations. In certain operations, such as a chemical plant, shower time may be compensable.

On-Call Time

Technology is rapidly changing the world in which we live. Employees are now accessible no matter where they are by pagers and cellular telephones. When does carrying a pager or being on-call require compensation? Compensation depends upon whether an employee can use the time for her benefit or whether the employer controls the time. The regulations use the terms "waiting to be engaged" (not compensable) and "engaged to wait" (compensable). If an employee can go to the mall, sit at home or attend a basketball game while on-call, the employee is "waiting to be engaged" and the time is generally not compensable.

Employees are "engaged to wait" if they are required to monitor radio communications and be within a certain distance of the worksite. Such time is compensable because an employee is not free to use the time for her own pleasure. Generally, if an employee is required to stay at home or at a fixed location to wait for calls, or if an employee is required to report at work within 20 minutes of receiving a call, the employee's time is so restricted that it will likely be treated as compensable in an enforcement action. Likewise, if the employee receives so many calls that they interrupt any normal personal activity, the on-call time will also be treated as compensable.

Waiting during working hours is sometimes an issue. The courts have held the following employees were entitled to compensation for waiting while on duty: 45 minutes of waiting time for assembly workers while the line was down, restaurant workers waiting for customers to arrive and employees who washed trucks who had to wait for the next one to arrive. The employees were not free to use the time for their own activities; therefore, the time was compensable.

Sample On-Call Policy

Employees will be "on-call" according to a schedule posted by the employer. While "on-call" employees are free to engage in personal pursuits such as going to restaurants, movies, amusement parks, etc., and are not required to remain in any particular location, an employee may not drink alcoholic beverages while on-call to the point where it would impair the ability to work and perform effectively if called.

Employees will be required to carry a paging device or "beeper" in order to be reached while on-call. Employees will be expected to report to the workplace within thirty (30) minutes after receiving a call. If personal circumstances arise so that an employee cannot be on-call when scheduled, the employer will attempt to arrange for substitute coverage or will attempt to allow extended response time as appropriate. If an employee receives an unusually high number of calls during the assigned on-call time, the employer will attempt to arrange a substitute, if requested.

THIS DOCUMENT HAS BEEN PREPARED BY ICE MILLER ONLY TO SERVE AS A GUIDE IN DEVELOPING AN APPROPRIATE POLICY OR AGREEMENT. AN EMPLOYER SHOULD CONSULT WITH COUNSEL CONCERNING HOW THIS GUIDE SHOULD BE USED IN LIGHT OF ANY PARTICULAR FACTUAL SITUATION, AND TO DISCUSS CHANGES WHICH MAY HAVE OCCURRED IN THE UNDERLYING LAW AND REGULATIONS.

Rest Periods and Meal Periods

Contrary to popular belief, the FLSA does not mandate break or meal periods. Some states require rest and meal periods, but Indiana is not one of them (different rules apply for minors). Nevertheless, breaks and meal periods are almost universally permitted, to increase efficiency and safety in the workplace. Breaks of 20 minutes or less are compensable. Whether meal periods (30 minutes or longer) are compensable is left to the employer's discretion. An employer may allow a paid or unpaid meal period. However, if the meal period is unpaid, an employee must be completely relieved of duties and free to leave his or her regular work area (however the employee may be required to remain on plant premises if a lunchroom or break room is available for eating). If an employee performs work during his or her unpaid lunch hour, the employer must compensate the employee (unless the work is de minimus). Compensation is also required if employees are required to eat at their desks or machines.

> **Example:** The employer has a well-established policy that forbids employees to work during their unpaid lunch hour. Employee Bob likes to sit at his desk and eat his lunch while "surfing the Internet." Is Bob entitled to compensation for his lunch hour? Answer: No. The "suffer or permit" doctrine is applicable only when an employee is performing work. "Surfing the Internet" is not performing work. An employer is not automatically required to pay an employee because he voluntarily remained at his desk during his lunch hour. The problem with permitting non-exempt employees to eat lunch at their desks is being able to distinguish between e-mailing friends (non-compensable) and editing a report (compensable). This is why many employers take an additional precaution and require employees to leave their workstations during lunch.

Training Programs Sponsored by the Employer

Time spent by employees at training sessions, lectures and meetings is not compensable if the following four factors are met:

   ♦ attendance is outside an employee's regular working hours;

- attendance is voluntary;

- attendance is not directly related to the employee's current job; and

- no productive activity is performed during attendance.

An employer is required to compensate employees for attending training programs if attendance is mandatory and/or the program is designed to assist employees in performing their current jobs. There is an exception, however, to the "directly related" criteria: many employees take classes offered by or equivalent to those offered by a college or university outside normal working hours, even if the employer pays tuition for the class; this time is not compensable under the FLSA.

If an employer offers an apprenticeship program, an employer may exclude the training from compensable work time if two requirements are met:

- the apprentice is employed under a written apprenticeship agreement or program that meets the standards under the Bureau of Apprenticeship and Training of the Department of Labor; and

- no productive time or performance of regular job duties are involved.

Compensability of Pre-Hire Training/Orientation Programs

The status of a pre-hire trainee is governed by factors derived from the United States Supreme Court's decision in *Walling v. Portland Terminal Company*, 330 U.S. 148 (1947). In that case, the Court considered a course of practical training offered by a railroad for prospective yard brakemen. The railroad did not guarantee employment to trainees; however, unless prospective brakemen completed the training and were certified as competent, they could not be placed in a pool from which qualified workmen were subsequently hired. The Court noted that the activities of these trainees did not displace any regular employees of the railroad, did not expedite the railroad's business and in fact actually sometimes impeded such activities, and that the training was similar to that offered by public or private vocational schools, primarily for the benefit of the trainees.

Based on this decision, the Department of Labor has identified six factors to be considered in determining whether trainees or students are employees of an employer under the Act, based on all the circumstances surrounding their activities on the premises of the employer:

- The training, even though it includes actual operation of the facilities of the employer, is similar to that which would be given in a vocational school.

- The training is for the benefit of the trainees or students.

- The trainees or students do not displace regular employees, but work under their close observation.

- The employer that provides the training derives no immediate advantage from the activities of the trainees or students; and on occasion its operations may actually be impeded.

- The trainees or students are not necessarily entitled to a job at the conclusion of the training period.

- The employer and the trainees or students understand that the trainees or students are not entitled to wages for the time spent in the training.

Travel Time

Several different situations arise regarding compensation for time spent traveling.

Home to Work

Employers are not required to compensate employees for travel from home to work. This is true even if an employee works at a fixed site or at different job sites. Additionally, the law does not require compensation for "walking, riding or traveling to and from the actual place of performance" of the principal work activity. For example: in downtown Indianapolis, parking costs are substantial. An employer secures a parking lot several miles from the worksite and provides a shuttle service for employees. Travel time on the shuttle is not considered compensable work time unless there is an express custom, practice or contract.

Travel During the Day

Travel during regular work hours from worksite to worksite is compensable. Occasionally, an employee works past his normal quitting time at a different site. The return trip to the original worksite is compensable time. The travel from worksite to home would not be compensable. Likewise, if the employee travels directly from the second worksite to home that travel is not compensable because it is considered ordinary home to work travel.

Home to Work in Emergencies

Compensation is required if, after regular work hours have ended, an employer requests an employee to travel a substantial distance to perform an emergency job. In this situation, all time spent on travel is working time.

Special One-Day Assignment

Management gives an employee who normally works in a fixed location a special one-day assignment to a different city. Since the travel benefits the employer and is at the employer's request, the time spent traveling is compensable. For example, an employee who works in Indianapolis with regular working hours from 9 a.m. – 5 p.m. has a one-day assignment in Evansville. The employee must report to Evansville at 9 a.m. Obviously, the employee must leave Indianapolis before 9 a.m. The time spent traveling to Evansville is hours worked. It is not ordinary home to work travel.

Travel for an Overnight Trip

Whether an employer is required to compensate for overnight travel depends upon when the travel occurs and the mode of transportation. The FLSA requires compensation for employees who are passengers on an airplane, train, boat or automobile on an overnight trip, only for time spent in travel that occurs during the employee's normal working hours, including what would be the normal working hours on non-working days, such as weekends and holidays. If an employee normally works from 9 a.m. to 5 p.m., then travel that occurs during those hours must be compensated, even on Saturday and Sunday. If an employee is required to drive a personal automobile, then all travel time is compensable even if it occurs outside the employee's normal working hours; however, if the employee is offered public transportation but requests permission to drive, then only actual driving time, or the time the employee would have spent traveling during normal hours by public conveyance, needs be compensated.

> **Example:** An employee who normally works 8 a.m. to 4 p.m. is required to attend a two-day conference in Chicago on Monday and Tuesday. The employee is offered public transportation, but departs on Sunday evening in her personal vehicle. After the conference ends at 3 p.m., the employee starts her return journey. What compensation is the employer required to provide? Answer: the employee is NOT entitled to compensation for time spent traveling on Sunday since it occurred outside her normal working

hours; the employee is entitled to compensation for time attending the conference on Monday and Tuesday since attendance was mandatory; one hour of time spent traveling on Tuesday is compensable, from 3 p.m. to 4 p.m., since it occurred during the employee's normal working hours.

Sample Policy for Compensation for Travel Time

Non-exempt employees will be compensated for time spent in travel according to the following guidelines:

1. Travel from home to work is not compensable. Such home to work travel time is not compensable whether the employee works at a fixed location or at different job sites within a normal commuting distance. Travel time to a special job site outside normal commuting distance will be counted as time worked.

2. After an employee has come to work, travel during the workday from one site to another will be counted as time worked.

3. An employee who receives a special assignment to travel out of town during a single workday will be compensated for travel time to and from the site of the special assignment.

4. [OPTION 1]   An employee whose work requires an overnight trip will be compensated for travel time to and from the overnight site that occurs during the employee's regular working hours, including the corresponding hours on non-working days. Travel in connection with an overnight trip that occurs outside the employee's regular working hours will not be compensated.

    [OPTION 2]   An employee whose work requires an overnight trip will be compensated for travel time to and from the overnight site which occurs during the employee's regular working hours, including the corresponding hours on nonworking days. Any travel outside the employee's regular working hours will also be compensated, but not if the employee's total travel, plus any work hours during that day, would exceed the number of hours in the employee's regular work day.

    [OPTION 3]   An employee whose work requires an overnight trip will be compensated for travel time to and from the overnight site, but compensated travel time will not exceed the number of hours in the employee's regular work day. Any work performed on a day of overnight travel will be compensated in addition to travel time.

    [OPTION 4]   An employee whose work requires an overnight trip will be compensated for travel time to and from the overnight site, in addition to compensation for any work performed.

    Employees will be provided public transportation for overnight trips. If an employee is permitted to use a personal vehicle, only hours the employee would have spent using public transportation will be counted under this policy. An employee who is required to travel by personal vehicle or to drive a company vehicle on an overnight trip will be compensated for all travel time.

THIS DOCUMENT HAS BEEN PREPARED BY ICE MILLER ONLY TO SERVE AS A GUIDE IN DEVELOPING AN APPROPRIATE POLICY OR AGREEMENT. AN EMPLOYER SHOULD CONSULT WITH COUNSEL CONCERNING HOW THIS GUIDE SHOULD BE USED IN LIGHT OF ANY PARTICULAR FACTUAL SITUATION, AND TO DISCUSS CHANGES WHICH MAY HAVE OCCURRED IN THE UNDERLYING LAW AND REGULATIONS.

Sleeping Time

Sleeping time may be broken into two categories: duty of less than 24 hours and duty of 24 hours or more.

Duty of Less than 24 Hours

Sleeping time is compensable for employees who work less than 24 hours. This is true even if the employer allows an employee to sleep or engage in personal activities while on duty during slow periods. As noted above, however, duty free meal periods of 30 minutes or longer need not be compensated.

Duty of 24 Hours or More

An employee and employer are free to agree that sleeping periods of not more than eight hours are not compensable provided:

- adequate sleeping facilities are provided; and

- the employee can enjoy uninterrupted sleep.

Absent express or implied agreement, sleep time is compensable. The Department of Labor's standard is that if an employee cannot obtain a minimum of five hours sleep, the entire time is compensable. Any time an employee is interrupted in his sleep, the interruption is compensable.

Medical Exams

Time spent by an employee waiting for or receiving medical attention either on the employer's premises, or if directed by the employer at an outside medical facility, constitutes compensable hours if this occurs during the employee's normal work hours. Time spent receiving medical treatment outside normal working hours, even for injuries received at work, is not compensable. If an employee is offered medical treatment on site for a work-related injury, but elects to have treatment off premises, the time spent receiving such treatment is not compensable.

Chapter 5

Payment of Wages

Minimum Wage—Overview

Once an employer has determined the hours that must be compensated for its non-exempt employees, it must assure that those employees receive at least the minimum wage and that they receive overtime pay for hours worked over 40 each week. This chapter will deal with the minimum wage and related wage payment obligations. The federal Minimum Wage Increase Act of 1996 increased the federal minimum wage to $5.15 an hour as of September 1, 1997. Indiana also has a state minimum wage law, Ind. Code § 22-2-2-1 et seq., which applies to employers who are not covered by the FLSA and who have two or more employees. Indiana's minimum wage was increased to $5.15 per hour in 1999. Increases in the minimum wage are politically charged, and the current minimum wage level is generally less than actually required to hire even entry level workers in today's labor market. However, Congress periodically does increase the minimum wage, sometimes with special provisions such as a training wage or other sub-minimum allowances, so this must be monitored carefully.

Minimum wage laws do not require an employer to pay an employee on an hourly basis, but instead require that the amount paid per hour during a workweek meets or exceeds the established minimum. For example, an employee may be paid on a salary, commission or piece-rate basis. However, this does not relieve the employer of its minimum wage obligations. The employer must divide the compensation paid for a given workweek by the number of hours worked by the employee during that workweek to determine the hourly wage paid for that week. If the hourly wage falls below the minimum, the employer must adopt the minimum wage rate for the employee for that week.

Certain employees may be paid less than the full minimum wage under the FLSA. These include student-learners enrolled in vocational education programs; full-time students employed in retail or service establishments, agriculture or institutions of higher education; and individuals whose earning or productive capacity is impaired by a physical or mental disability. Certificates issued by the U.S. Department of Labor are required for this type of sub-minimum wage employment.

Under both federal and state law, a minimum wage of not less than $4.25 per hour may be paid to employees under the age of 20 for their first 90 consecutive calendar days of employment with any employer as long as their work does not displace other workers. After 90 consecutive days of employment, or when the worker reaches age 20, whichever comes first, the worker must receive the minimum wage of $5.15 per hour.

Non-Cash Payments Treated as Wages

The FLSA defines the term "wage" to include the "reasonable cost" to an employer of furnishing an employee with board, lodging or "other facilities," if such board, lodging or other facilities are customarily furnished by the employer to its employees. Thus, the FLSA permits employers to include the reasonable cost of board, lodging or other facilities customarily furnished to their employees in order to fulfill their minimum wage obligations. The reasonable cost cannot exceed the fair market value of the board, lodging or other facilities provided, and cannot include any profit earned by the employer. The employee's acceptance of the board, lodging or other facilities must be voluntary and uncoerced.

Board and lodging are clear enough, but the term "other facilities" requires some elaboration. DOL describes "other facilities" this way: "Other facilities" must be something like board or lodging. The following items have been deemed to be within the meaning of the term:

- Meals furnished at company restaurants or cafeterias or by hospitals, hotels or restaurants to their employees.

- Meals, dormitory rooms and tuition furnished by a college to its student employees.

- Housing furnished for dwelling purposes.

- General merchandise furnished at company stores and commissaries (including articles of food, clothing and household effects).

- Fuel (including coal, kerosene, firewood and lumber slabs), electricity, water and gas furnished for the noncommercial personal use of the employee.

- Transportation furnished employees between their homes and work in which the travel time does not constitute hours worked compensable under the Act and the transportation is not an incident of and necessary to the employment.

The cost of board, lodging or other facilities cannot be included as part of an employee's wages if excluded by a bona fide collective bargaining agreement. The cost also cannot be included as wages if the employer furnishes the facilities primarily for its own benefit or convenience. Examples of facilities that have been found to be primarily for the benefit or convenience of the employer include tools of the trade and other materials incidental to carrying on the employer's business, as well as the costs of uniforms and their laundering, in which the nature of the business requires the employee to wear a uniform.

If an employer provides non-cash compensation, the reasonable costs of such non-cash compensation must be included in computing the regular hourly rate for the purpose of overtime, which is discussed in Chapter 6.

Impermissible Deductions

As noted above, the cost of facilities that are provided primarily for the employer's benefit, which includes the cost of uniforms and of their laundering in which the nature of the business requires the employee to wear a uniform, cannot be included as wages. By the same token, if the employer requires an employee to pay this cost, the payment is treated as a deduction from the employee's pay. If that deduction results in the employee receiving less than the minimum wage, the deduction is not permitted and a minimum wage violation has occurred.

This problem has occurred in the restaurant industry, as employers have provided uniforms, but have required employees to launder the uniforms on their own time and at their own expense. If those employees are paid the bare minimum wage, the employer has been found liable for the reasonable cost of laundering and an estimate of the time spent by the employee performing this task. If, however, the employee is paid sufficiently more than minimum wage to cover this cost, there is no liability. A similar calculation is required if an employee is required to pay for tools and/or other supplies necessary for carrying out the employer's business, to pay for transportation required by the employer as a necessary part of employment or to pay for any other normal and customary business expense of the employer.

Tips and Tip Credit

An employer of a tipped employee is only required to pay $2.13 an hour in direct wages if that amount plus the tips received equals at least the federal minimum wage; the employee does not turn over any of the tips to the employer; and the employee customarily and regularly receives more than $30 a month in tips. If an employee's tips combined with the employer's direct wages of at least $2.13 an hour do not equal the federal minimum hourly wage, the employer must make up the difference. If an employee receives more in tips than the difference between the minimum wage and $2.13 per hour, the credit remains the same and the employer still must pay $2.13 per hour in cash wages.

To determine if a tip credit can be taken, an employer must consider:

- which payments constitute tips;

- whether the employee receives more than $30 per month in such payments in the occupation in which he or she is engaged; and

- if in such occupation he or she receives such payments "customarily and regularly."

A tip is defined by the regulations as a sum presented by a customer as a gift or gratuity in recognition of some service performed for him or her. Tips must be paid in cash or its equivalent, and include amounts transferred by the employer to the employee pursuant to directions from credit card customers who designate a sum to be added to their bill as a tip. By contrast, compulsory service charges, such as a 15 percent gratuity imposed on the customer's bill by the establishment, are not tips but gross receipts to the employer. The employer may utilize such income however chosen, including using the service charge to pay employees of the establishment. Regardless of how the service charge is used, it is considered to be non-tip income for statutory purposes. Therefore, if the employer traditionally adds a 15 percent or more gratuity to every bill generated, each of the employees must be paid an hourly rate equal to the minimum wage.

The tip credit applies only to tipped employees, and the employee must be informed about the provisions of the tip credit. A tipped employee is one who is engaged in an occupation in which he or she "customarily and regularly" receives more than $30 a month in tips. The tip credit provision applies on an individual basis. The fact that the employee is part of a group that has a record of receiving more than $30 a month in tips will not qualify the employee for the tip credit. The employer may therefore claim the tip credit for some employees even though the claim cannot be made for other employees.

If an employee has dual jobs, such as a hotel maintenance person who also works as a waiter, a tip credit can be taken for the hours worked as a waiter if the tip credit requirements are met, but no tip credit can be taken for the hours worked as a maintenance person. The regulations state that this situation can be distinguished from that of a waitress who spends part of her time cleaning and setting tables, toasting bread, making coffee and occasionally washing glasses. Although these are not duties that are directed toward producing tips, the regulations describe them as related duties in an occupation that is a tipped occupation.

Not only must the employer advise the employee of the tip credit in order to take advantage of it, but the employer must also allow employees to retain all tips received. A tip is the property of the employee in recognition of the service provided to a customer; it cannot become the property of the employer without losing its character as a tip. Thus, if tips are turned over to the employer as part of gross receipts, no tip credit can be taken and the minimum wage must be paid in full.

Nevertheless, tipped employees may split or pool tips among themselves. A valid tip pooling arrangement includes only employees who customarily and regularly receive tips. In addition, tipped employees cannot be required to contribute an unreasonable percentage of their tips to the pool.

Timing of Wage Payments

Wage payments must be made on the regular payday for each workweek. When a pay period covers more than a single week, payment of all wages must be made on the regular payday for the workweek in which the pay period ends. In almost all cases, Indiana employers must pay their employees at least semimonthly or biweekly, but only if the employee so requests. Paydays may not be scheduled more than 10 days after the end of the regularly scheduled pay period. Payments must be made in lawful money of the United States, by negotiable check, draft or money order, or by electronic transfer to the financial institution designated by the employee.

If an employee is discharged or voluntarily leaves employment, the employer is not required to pay the employee the amount due the employee until the next usual and regular day for payment of wages, as established by the employer. This is also the case if work is suspended as a result of an industrial dispute.

Failure to pay employees their wages in a timely manner, whether during employment or thereafter, can expose the employer to a lawsuit for lost wages, punitive damages, costs and attorney's fees. Pursuant to Indiana Code § 22-2-5-2, employers are required to pay a penalty of 10 percent of the amount due per day until the penalty reaches double the amount of damages. Combining the damages for actual lost wages with the mandatory punitive damages, the statute can result in an award of triple damages to the former employee. In addition, the former employee is entitled to recover costs and reasonable attorney's fees. If an employee leaves voluntarily and without the employee's address or whereabouts being known to the employer, the employer is not subject to penalties under Indiana Code § 22-2-5-2 until:

- 10 days have elapsed after the employee has made a demand for the wages due; or

- the employee has furnished the employer with the employee's address where the wages may be forwarded.

Wage Assignments

Permissible Wage Assignments

Indiana only allows deductions to be made from wages for certain enumerated reasons and only if certain express procedural safeguards are met. Deductions made from an employee's wages generally are defined as "wage assignments." See Ind. Code § 22-2-6-1(a) ("Any direction given by an employee to an employer to make a deduction from the wages to be earned by said employee, after said direction is given, shall constitute an assignment of the wages of said employee.")

An assignment of the wages of an employee is valid only if the assignment is:

- in writing;

- signed by the employee personally;

- by its terms revocable at any time by the employee upon written notice to the employer; and

- agreed to in writing by the employer. In addition, an executed copy of the assignment must be delivered to the employer within 10 days after its execution.

Furthermore, a wage assignment may be made only for the purpose of paying the following:

- Premium on a policy of insurance obtained for the employee by the employer.

- Pledge or contribution of the employee to a charitable or nonprofit organization.

- Purchase price of bonds or securities, issued or guaranteed by the United States.

- Purchase price of shares of stock, or fractional interests therein, of the employing company, or of a company owning the majority of the issued and outstanding stock of the employing company, whether purchased from such company, in the open market or otherwise. However, if such shares are to be purchased on installments pursuant to a written purchase agreement, the employee has the right under the purchase agreement at any time before completing purchase of such shares to cancel said agreement and to have repaid promptly the amount of all installment payments that theretofore have been made.

- Dues by the employee to a labor organization of which the employee is a member.

- Purchase price of merchandise sold by the employer to the employee, at the written request of the employee.

- Amount of a loan made to the employee by the employer and evidenced by a written instrument executed by the employee subject to the amount limits set forth in Indiana Code § 22-2-6-4(c).

- Contributions, assessments or dues of the employee to a hospital service or a surgical or medical expense plan or to an employees' association, trust or plan existing for the purpose of paying pensions or other benefits to said employee or to others designated by the employee.

- Payment to any credit union, nonprofit organizations or associations of employees of such employer organized under any law of Indiana or the United States.

- Payment to any person or organization regulated under the Uniform Consumer Credit Code for deposit or credit to the employee's account by electronic transfer or as otherwise designated by the employee.

- Premiums on policies of insurance and annuities purchased by the employee on the employee's life.

- The purchase price of shares or fractional interest in shares in one or more mutual funds.

- A judgment owed by the employee if the payment is made in accordance with an agreement between the employee and the creditor and is not a garnishment under Indiana Code § 34-25-3.

Fines Prohibited

It is unlawful for any employer to assess a fine against an employee and to deduct the amount of the fine from the employee's wages for any reason.

Deductions for Overpayment of Wages

If an employer has overpaid an employee, the employer may deduct the amount of the overpayment from the wages of the employee. Before doing so, however, the employer must give the employee two weeks notice. In addition, the employer may not deduct from an employee's wages an amount in dispute. A deduction by an employer for reimbursement of an overpayment of wages previously made to an employee is not considered to be a fine or an assignment of wages.

When an employer makes a deduction for an overpayment from the employee's wages, the employer may not be able to withhold the entire amount from a single paycheck. Employers are restricted from deducting any amount greater than 25 percent of the employee's disposable earnings or the amount by which the employee's disposable earnings exceed 30 times the minimum wage rate, whichever is smaller. However, an employer may deduct the entire amount of a single gross wage overpayment if that overpayment was 10 times the employee's gross wages due to a misplaced decimal point.

Rounding Practices Permitted and Penalties Prohibited

The DOL regulations recognize that employers may engage in rounding practices, *i.e.*, recording an employee's starting and stopping times to the nearest five minutes, one-tenth of an hour or one-quarter of an hour. This arrangement must average out so that the employees are fully compensated for all the time they actually work. For enforcement purposes, this practice of computing working time will be accepted by the DOL provided that it is used in such a manner that it will not result, over a period of time, in failure to compensate the employees properly for all the time they have actually worked. In other words, the rounding must go up roughly as often as it goes down. It is NOT permissible to arbitrarily disregard an entire tenth of an hour, for example, if the employee fails to work that entire tenth.

The regulations also state that if time clocks are used, employees who voluntarily come in before their regular starting time or remain after their closing time do not have to be paid for such periods provided that they do not engage in any work. Although minor differences between clock records and actual hours worked cannot ordinarily be avoided, major discrepancies should be discouraged since they raise a doubt as to the accuracy of the records of the hours actually worked. As an enforcement policy, DOL typically does not question records that show a clock-in time up to 15 minutes before the actual starting time, but DOL will carefully review any greater difference. This may include interviews of the employees to determine if any work was actually performed.

Vacation Pay

In Indiana, unless an employer has a written policy to the contrary, a terminated employee is entitled to be paid for accrued but unused vacation. "Since vacation pay is additional wages, earned weekly, where only the time of payment is deferred, it necessarily follows that, absent an agreement to the contrary, the employee would be entitled to a pro rata share at the time of termination." *Die & Mold v. Western*, 448 N.E.2d 44, 48 (Ind. Ct. App. 1983).

Following Die & Mold, it is important for employers to carefully craft the language of their vacation policies. If an employer wants to limit the circumstances under which payments are made for unused vacation time, then the employer needs to adopt a clear policy. If an employer does not want to provide any vacation pay to employees upon separation of employment, the employer's policy should specifically provide for this. Moreover, if employees cannot carry over vacation (*i.e.*, the company has a "use it or lose it" policy), the employer should say so in its policy.

In *Indiana Heart Associates, P.C. v. Bahamonde*, 714 N.E.2d 309, 311, 312-13 (Ind. Ct. App. 1999), transfer denied, 735 N.E.2d 220 (Ind. 2000), the court held that an employer could deny an employee accrued vacation or paid time off (PTO) pay to which the employee would otherwise be entitled on the basis of a written policy, but the employer bears the burden of showing a violation of that policy. In *Bahamonde*, the employer had terminated the employee for alleged gross misconduct. The employer's written policy said that an employee would not be eligible for payment of any PTO time if the employee was involuntarily terminated for, among other things, "gross misconduct." However, the policy did not define gross misconduct, and there were fact issues as to whether the employee's alleged conduct fell within that description.

Vacation pay is considered to be wages within the meaning of the Indiana Wage Payment and Wage Claims statutes. This means that failure to pay vacation pay when due can subject the employer to a claim for treble damages, costs and attorney's fees under Ind. Code § 22-2-5-2.

Commissions and Bonuses

Commissions are also "wages" within the meaning of the Wage Payment and Wage Claims statutes. When an individual leaves employment, the employer must pay the departing employee commissions that the employee has earned to the date of termination. Issues often arise as to whether a commission has been earned and whether an employee is entitled to trailing commissions. Therefore, it is important that the employer have a clearly stated policy or written agreement with the employee that explains how and when commissions are earned.

Depending upon their purpose, bonuses may or may not be considered wages within the meaning of the Wage Payment and Wage Claims statutes. Absent an agreement to the contrary, an employer generally is not obligated to pay any part of a discretionary bonus to a departing employee. However, if the bonus is not discretionary, but is linked to time worked or the amount of work done, such a bonus likely will be considered wages and could activate a claim under the Wage Payment and Wage Claims statutes. Commissions and non-discretionary bonuses must also be included in calculating overtime, as discussed in Chapter 6.

Chapter 6

Calculation of Overtime

Determining the Workweek

There is no limitation in the Fair Labor Standards Act (other than child labor provisions) on the number of hours that an employee may work in a workweek. However, unless specifically exempted, the FLSA requires employers to pay employees overtime pay for hours worked in excess of 40 hours in a workweek. Overtime pay is paid at a rate of not less than one and one-half times the employee's regular rate of pay for each hour worked over the maximum hour standard in a workweek. The FLSA does not require overtime pay for hours worked over eight in a day or over the normal daily hours scheduled, or for hours worked on Saturdays, Sundays, holidays or regular days of rest. Employers may elect to pay overtime for such hours and if so, the overtime paid counts toward the employer's basic obligation to pay for overtime over 40 hours each week.

In most cases employees must be paid overtime for hours worked in excess of 40 in a single established workweek. For purposes of the FLSA, an employee's workweek is a fixed and regularly reoccurring period of 168 hours comprising seven consecutive 24-hour periods. The workweek may begin on any day of the week, at any time, and need not coincide with the calendar week. In addition, employers may establish different workweeks for different plants, employees or groups of employees. Employers must communicate to employees when the workweek begins and ends. An employer may change a workweek only if it intends for the change to be permanent and does not make the change in order to circumvent overtime requirements.

Overtime calculation under the single workweek method applies regardless of whether the employee is paid on a daily, weekly, bi-weekly, semi-monthly or monthly basis, or whether the employee is paid on a piecework or commission basis. Normally, overtime pay earned in a particular workweek must be paid on the regular payday for the pay period in which the wages were earned. If overtime cannot be determined when the pay period ends, the employer has a grace period for the computation and payment. Payment must be paid by the next payday after the computation reasonably can be made.

Employers have the discretion to determine whether nonworking hours (*i.e.*, holidays, sick days) count as hours worked for overtime calculations. Employers should establish a policy to notify employees whether non-working hours (holidays, sick days, etc.) will count as hours worked for overtime purposes.

> **Example**: Paul worked the following schedule:
>
> | | |
> |---|---|
> | Monday | 8 hours |
> | Tuesday | 8 hours |
> | Wednesday | 8 hours |
> | Thursday | Christmas (did not work, but received 8 hours of holiday pay) |
> | Friday | 8 hours |
> | Saturday | 8 hours |
> | Sunday | 8 hours |
>
> Pursuant to the FLSA, the employer must pay Paul 40 hours of pay at his regular rate, plus eight hours of overtime at the rate of 1½ times his regular rate. In addition, if the employer, in its discretion, designated Christmas day as a holiday that counts as hours worked for overtime calculations, the employer must pay Paul 40 hours of pay at his regular rate of pay, plus 16 hours of overtime at the rate of 1½ times his regular rate.

Exceptions to the Single Workweek Rule

Certain employers are permitted to calculate overtime over a period longer than a single workweek. Hospitals and nursing homes may reach an agreement or understanding with some or all of their employees to pay employees overtime under the "8 and 80" plan. Under this plan, the employer pays overtime for hours worked over eight hours in a day and more than 80 hours in a 14-day period. An understanding for this purpose is reached if the employee knowingly accepts payment of wages after receiving notification that the employer will pay under the "8 and 80" plan. In the absence of such an understanding, overtime must be paid for hours worked over 40 in a single workweek.

Overtime pay for publicly employed firefighters and law enforcement personnel, including prison security personnel, may be calculated using up to a 28-day work period rather than a single workweek. An agreement or understanding is NOT required although the public employer must keep accurate records showing the work period and hours worked for each covered employee. The number of hours at which overtime is required in a 28-day work period is 212 for fire protection activities and 171 for law enforcement activities. What constitutes compensable time for police and fire employees is defined using a special standard, referred to as a "tour of duty" in regulations of the Department of Labor.

Calculating the Regular Rate of Pay

Employers are required by the FLSA to pay covered employees 1½ times their "regular rate" for each hour, or fraction thereof, worked in excess of 40 during any given workweek. Before properly calculating overtime pay, the employer must determine exactly what the "regular rate" is. Computation of the regular rate takes two steps. First, the employee's compensation must be reviewed to determine which amounts must be included in the regular rate. Then, the employee's total weekly remuneration is converted to an hourly rate.

The regular rate of pay is NOT necessarily just the employee's base hourly rate. The regular rate includes ALL remuneration for employment paid to, or on behalf of, the employee, except for certain types of payments the statute specifically exempts. For example, bonuses, commission payments, payments for meals, lodging and facilities, shift differentials, hazardous duty premiums, cost-of-living allowances, on-call pay and tip credits, etc., are considered remuneration for work performed and must be included in the regular rate computation.

If non-cash payments are made to employees in the form of goods or facilities, the reasonable cost to the employer or fair value of such goods or facilities must be included in the regular rate. In other words, overtime is required on both cash and non-cash compensation received. For example, if an employee received minimum wage (currently $5.15 per hour) but also receives meals each day from the employer, the reasonable cost of which is equivalent of to 50 cents per hour, then the employee's regular rate for the purpose of overtime is $5.65, and an employer must pay time and one-half that rate for hours worked over 40 each week. Non-cash wages may be excluded from this calculation if they are excluded from wages under a union contract. On-the-job sleeping facilities provided for the benefit of the employer are not included.

Some other payments are specifically excluded from the regular rate such as discretionary bonuses, gifts, and certain employee benefit plan contributions.

If an employee in a single workweek works two or more different types of work for which different straight-time rates have been established, the regular rate for that week is normally calculated using the same principle – the earnings from all such rates are added together and this total is then divided by the total number of hours worked at all jobs. Likewise, if an employer pays earnings on a piece rate, salary, commission or other basis, the overtime pay due is computed on the basis of the average hourly rate derived from all such earnings. In most cases, a commission or piecework employee's regular rate of pay is computed by dividing his or her total remuneration (incentive and base) for the workweek by the number of hours actually worked during the workweek.

The FLSA provides that an agreement may be reached for employees who work at two or more different jobs during the week at different hourly rates to compute overtime based on the hourly rate in effect when the overtime is worked, if the hourly rate is a bona fide rate that would be paid to employees performing the work on a straight time basis and certain other conditions are met. Determining what constitutes overtime in this situation is critical, and care must be taken to develop a plan which meets all the legal requirements. (The same type of agreement may be reached to permit paying a piecework employee overtime based on time and one-half the piece rate in effect when the overtime occurs, as discussed later in this chapter.)

SAMPLE AGREEMENT TWO JOBS WITH DIFFERENT PAY

Overtime Based On Weighted-Average Rate

This letter is intended to serve as a memorandum of our mutual understanding regarding compensation for your employment with _____. You will be employed to perform two different jobs: (1) _____ for which you will receive a straight time hourly rate of $_____ (not less than minimum wage); and (2) _____ for which you will receive a straight time hourly rate of $_____ (not less than minimum wage).

For all overtime hours worked, you will be paid the straight time hourly rate for the job you are actually performing during such overtime hours, plus an additional overtime premium equal to one-half of your weighted-average hourly rate for the week. Your weighted-average hourly rate will equal your total straight time pay for the week divided by the total number of hours worked.

We request that you indicate your understanding and acceptance of this arrangement by your signature in the space indicated.

_____   _____

Employer   Employee

SAMPLE AGREEMENT TWO JOBS WITH DIFFERENT PAY
Overtime Based on the Rate in Effect
When Overtime Hours are Worked

This letter is intended to serve as a memorandum of our mutual understanding regarding compensation for your employment with _____. You will be employed to perform two different jobs: (1) _____ for which you will receive a straight time hourly rate of $_____ (not less than minimum wage); and (2) _____ for which you will receive a straight time hourly rate of $_____ (not less than minimum wage). For all overtime hours worked, you will be paid one and one-half times the straight time hourly rate for the job you are actually performing during such overtime hours. Hours actually worked over forty (40) in your established workweek will constitute overtime hours.

OPTIONAL: For the purpose of this agreement only, the following hours will also be considered overtime hours:

- Any hours worked on Saturday, Sunday or holidays (unless such days occur during the employee's normal workweek).

- Any hours worked on your regular days of rest.

- Any hours worked on the sixth or seventh day of your workweek.

- Any hours worked in excess of eight in a day.

- Any hours worked outside your normal established workday of _____ hours (not exceeding eight).

- Any hours worked outside your normal established workweek of _____ hours (not exceeding forty).

We request that you indicate your understanding and acceptance of this arrangement by your signature in the space indicated.

_____   _____
Employer   Employee

THIS DOCUMENT HAS BEEN PREPARED BY ICE MILLER ONLY TO SERVE AS A GUIDE IN DEVELOPING AN APPROPRIATE POLICY OR AGREEMENT. AN EMPLOYER SHOULD CONSULT WITH COUNSEL CONCERNING HOW THIS GUIDE SHOULD BE USED IN LIGHT OF ANY PARTICULAR FACTUAL SITUATION, AND TO DISCUSS CHANGES WHICH MAY HAVE OCCURRED IN THE UNDERLYING LAW AND REGULATIONS.

Example: Sam, the company's longstanding maintenance employee, makes $15 per hour. The company normally uses an outside service to mow the grass during the summer; however, Sam has asked to do this work on the weekend for a flat $50. It would normally take Sam about two hours to complete this work.

It is unlikely that the company could successfully contend that Sam is an "independent contractor" with respect to the mowing work, since he is not normally in the business of mowing for other customers and is not established as a mowing business. (The fact that this is secondary to the company's principal operations, and that the company has used an outside contractor previously, would weigh against this conclusion; however, DOL presumes that all work performed by an employee is included within the employment relationship, and it is very difficult to establish otherwise.)

Assuming that Sam is not an independent contractor and the mowing is considered part of his regular employment, a record must be made of hours worked in the mowing operation. If Sam works more than 40 hours, including the hours spent mowing, he will be entitled to overtime. How to compute the overtime is the problem.

Option 1—Weighted Average: Let's assume Sam works 45 hours in a given week, including the two hours spent mowing. In the absence of any special understanding, Sam's overtime would be calculated like this:

- $15.00 per hour x 43 maintenance = $645 regular straight time earnings, plus

- $50 for two hours of mowing, equals $695 total straight time compensation,

- $695 divided by 45 hours worked produces a $15.45 weighted average hourly rate.

One-half of the weighted average hourly rate times five overtime hours equals $38.63 additional overtime. (Sam has received time and one-half his regular hourly rate since he receives the full straight-time compensation for both types of work, plus an additional half-time premium, which amounts to time and one-half.)

Sam and the company could agree to a lower hourly rate for the mowing operation, since he will usually receive additional overtime. However, the time spent doing mowing must be accurately recorded, and Sam must receive only the lower rate if, in fact, he works less than 40 hours and there is no overtime involved. Because the hourly rate for mowing is greater than Sam's regular hourly rate for maintenance work, this method tends to inflate the rate at which overtime is paid.

Option 2—Rate in Effect When Work is Performed: This method would permit the company to continue to pay Sam overtime based on his regular maintenance rate for any overtime performed on maintenance work, but would then require that overtime be paid at time and one-half the hourly rate for his mowing work, which would be a larger figure for that overtime. This method requires that the rate paid for mowing be the bona fide rate the company would normally pay an employee to perform this work during only straight time hours. Also, the company can only treat the mowing work as overtime if it fits into a permitted category that the company has otherwise defined as overtime, *i.e.*, hours worked over 40, hours worked over eight in a day, hours worked on Saturday, Sunday or a holiday, etc. An agreement should be signed to implement this option. (See sample agreement listing the permitted categories of overtime).

Bonuses

Bonuses and incentive payments, dependent on the quality, quantity or efficiency of production, generally must be included in the regular rate of pay. Examples of such bonuses include:

- Production or work incentive bonuses. For example, bonuses that employers provide in order to induce employees to work faster or more efficiently, or to entice them to remain with the company, must be included in the regular rate of pay.

- Bonuses that are based on a percentage of sales.

- Cost of living bonuses.

- "Guaranteed wage" bonuses paid in order to bring employees up to a specified wage.

- Stock bonus plans.

- Attendance bonuses.

- Individual or group production bonuses.

- Bonuses for quality and accuracy of work.

- Bonuses, including lump sum bonuses negotiated as part of a collective bargaining agreement, which are contingent upon the employee's continuing in employment until the time payment is to be made.

Alternatively, a bonus may be excluded from the regular rate of pay if the bonus is purely discretionary. In other words, the employer must retain discretion both as to the fact of payment and the amount of the payment in order to exclude the bonus from the regular rate of pay. The amount of the bonus must be determined by the employer without any prior promises or agreements. The employee must not have any contract right, express or implied, to any fixed sum. Thus, if an employer promises in advance to pay a bonus, it has abandoned its discretion with regard to it. Such a bonus would be included in the regular rate of pay.

If a bonus, which must be included in the regular rate of pay, covers only one pay period, the amount of the bonus is added to the other earnings of the employee and the total is divided by the total hours worked in order to obtain the regular rate of pay. The employee is entitled to this rate for each of the first 40 hours and to 1½ times this rate for each additional hour worked over 40. When a bonus is paid less often than weekly, the amount of the bonus must be allocated back over the period of time it covers. This is done by dividing the amount of the bonus by the number of hours worked by the employee in the period covered by the bonus. Then, for each overtime hour worked in the period, the employee is given an additional amount equal to ½ the hourly bonus figure. If it is impossible to determine the amount of the bonus actually earned each week, some other reasonable or equitable method of allocation must be used. For example, employers sometimes allocate an equal portion to each workweek, or alternatively to each hour worked.

Percentage of Wage Bonuses

If a bonus is calculated and paid as a percentage of the employee's total earnings, including both straight time and overtime earnings, the bonus satisfies the overtime obligation, since the percentage is applied to the employee's overtime pay and thus automatically includes time and one-half for overtime hours. Such a bonus must not be conditioned on continued employment during the future – in that case the bonus would be treated as part of the employee's compensation for future work as an incentive for such work and would have to be included in the regular hourly rate for the future period covered.

The percentage of wage bonus may be paid as a flat fixed percentage applied to each employee's total earnings, *e.g.* each employee receives five percent of his total earnings as a percentage of wage bonus. Or, an employer may create a "bonus pool" based on sales, profits, productivity or any other factor, which is shared by the affected employees based on their total compensation. Each employee would receive a percentage of the bonus pool which is the same as the percentage of that employee's total earnings to the total earnings of all employees participating in the bonus pool. It is not necessary to include all employees in the bonus pool, nor is there any limitation in how the overall amount of the bonus pool is established.

PERCENTAGE OF WAGE BONUS PLAN

We are pleased to announce that circumstances may permit the company to pay a monthly incentive bonus, which would be in addition to each employees regular wage earnings.

The monthly incentive bonus would be determined as follows. We would create a "bonus pool" at the end of each month, which would be ____ percent of the amount by which the company's (gross or net sales/productivity/other) exceed $ (specified total) . Each employee would get a "share" of the bonus pool that is equal to the percentage of that employee's total compensation for the month to the total compensation of all employees (in the plant/unit production unit). In other words, each employee's "share" of the bonus pool is the same as his or her "share" of our total compensation in this group for the month.

Please understand that the company cannot guarantee that any bonus will be paid in any given month, and the company must retain complete discretion about whether to pay a bonus in any month and about how much the bonus will be. This policy is not intended to create an obligation on the part of the company, but rather is an opportunity to share in the results when all of our hard work produces good results.

THIS DOCUMENT HAS BEEN PREPARED BY ICE MILLER ONLY TO SERVE AS A GUIDE IN DEVELOPING AN APPROPRIATE POLICY OR AGREEMENT. AN EMPLOYER SHOULD CONSULT WITH COUNSEL CONCERNING HOW THIS GUIDE SHOULD BE USED IN LIGHT OF ANY PARTICULAR FACTUAL SITUATION, AND TO DISCUSS CHANGES WHICH MAY HAVE OCCURRED IN THE UNDERLYING LAW AND REGULATIONS.

It is absolutely essential that the percentage of wage bonus be based on total compensation, including overtime pay. This often seems unfair to the employer. Employees who are inefficient and require overtime to complete their work end up receiving MORE bonus than employees who complete the same work without requiring overtime hours. Elimination of overtime from the calculation is NOT an option if the percentage of wage bonus plan is used. (Nor is it permissible to pay a bonus that varies in amount to artificially make up the difference between an employee's hourly earnings and some predetermined fixed amount. This is referred to as a "pseudo-bonus" designed to evade an employer's overtime obligation and expressly recognized and prohibited in regulations of the Department of Labor.)

Piecework

In certain jobs, employees may be paid on the basis of the number of units they produce. These employees are commonly called piece rate workers. In order to calculate the regular rate for piece rate workers, weekly earnings from piece rate and all other sources, such as production bonuses, sums paid for waiting or other hours worked, are totaled. This sum is then divided by the number of hours worked by the employee during the week. The result is the regular rate, which may not be less than the statutory minimum rate. Thus, if the employee worked a total of 50 hours and earned $245.50 at piece rates for 46 hours of productive work, and $5 an hour for four hours of waiting time, his total compensation, $265.50, must be divided by his total hours of work, 50, to provide a regular rate of pay of $5.31. The employee is paid 10 hours of overtime at $2.65 per hour. Alternatively, employers may pay employees overtime at an hourly rate equal to 1½ times the piece rate provided that the employee agrees, in advance, to this arrangement and the compensation is at least equal to 1½ times the minimum rate. In some instances, employers may pay a piece rate coupled with a minimum hourly guarantee. If the employee's total piece rate earnings for the workweek fall short of the amount that they would earn at the guaranteed rate, the employer pays the difference. In such weeks, the guaranteed rate, which must be at least equal to the statutory minimum wage, becomes the regular rate.

Commissions

Commissions are also considered payment for hours worked and must be included in the regular rate of pay. In order to obtain the regular rate for employees paid a weekly commission, the weekly commission payment is added to all other earnings for the week, and the total is divided by the hours worked in the workweek. However, if commissioned payments are deferred beyond the week in which they are earned, an employer must apportion the commissions back over the workweeks during which it was earned. Where appropriate, an employer may accomplish this by allocating an equal portion to each workweek, or to each hour worked.

Exclusions from the Regular Rate of Pay

Special rules allow employers to exclude from an employee's regular rate certain payments that are not measured by or dependent on hours worked, production or efficiency. These statutory exceptions include:

- Suggestion plan awards, if certain conditions are met.

- Discretionary bonuses, if both the fact and the amount of the payment are determined at the sole discretion of the employer.

- Employee referral bonuses.

- Payments made to a bona fide profit-sharing plan or trust or bona fide thrift or savings plan, if certain requirements are met.

- Gifts. For example, payments made in the nature of Christmas gifts, or on other special occasions as a reward for service, as long as the gift amount is not measured by hours worked, production or efficiency.

- Call-back pay and or show-up pay.

- Paid leave from work; for example, payments made for occasional periods when no work is performed due to vacation, holiday, illness, failure of the employer to provide sufficient work or other similar cause

- Reimbursement of expenses. For example, reasonable payments for traveling or other expenses, and other similar payments which are not made as compensation for hours worked are not included in the regular rate of pay.

- Talent fees paid to performers including announcers for radio and television programs.

- Contributions made to bona fide fringe benefit programs (bona fide plans for providing old age, retirement, life, accident, or health insurance or similar benefits for employees), if certain requirements are met.

- Premium overtime pay.

- Premium rate paid for work on Saturdays, Sundays, holidays, or regular days of rest, or on the sixth or seventh day of the workweek, if the premium rate is not less than 1½ times the rate established for like work performed in non-overtime hours on other days.

- Extra compensation provided by a premium rate paid pursuant to an employment contract or collective bargaining agreement, for work outside of the hours established by the contract or agreement as the regular workday or workweek if the premium is not less than 1½ times the rate established by the contract or agreement for like work performed during the workday or workweek.

The employer carries the burden of proving that a payment made to the employee falls within one of the exceptions. Although a payment may fall within one of the statutory exceptions, an employer is not required to exclude it.

Salaried Employees

An employer is free to pay both exempt and non-exempt employees on a salaried basis. **To repeat:** salaried employees are NOT automatically exempt from overtime – all of the requirements described in Chapter 3 must be satisfied; paying on a salaried basis is only one requirement and the primary duty tests must also be satisfied to qualify for a white collar exemption.

For non-exempt employees, overtime must be paid in addition to the salary for any hours worked over 40 in each workweek. How overtime is calculated (for salaried non-exempt employees) depends on what hours are worked that the salary is intended to cover. It is important to clearly establish exactly what hours are covered by a non-exempt employee's salary with a clearly defined policy disseminated to each affected employee, or by an express agreement or understanding with those employees.

Fixed Salary for Fixed Hours

In many cases, employees are paid a fixed weekly or bi-weekly salary which is intended to compensate for a fixed number of hours worked in a weekly or biweekly period. In this situation, the "regular rate" is the fixed salary for the established workweek divided by the fixed weekly hours. If the employee's fixed hours are less than 40, the employee is usually entitled to straight time for hours worked up to 40, and time and one-half the regular rate for hours worked over 40. When the fixed weekly hours are less than 40, hours worked between the fixed weekly schedule and 40 are sometimes referred to as "gap time."

SAMPLE GAP TIME AGREEMENT (Compensated)

This letter is intended to serve as a memo of our mutual understanding regarding compensation for your employment with_____. You will be employed as _____ at the _____ facility.

Effective _____, 20___, we will compensate you on the basis of a fixed weekly salary for up to thirty-five (35) hours worked in each workweek. Your regular scheduled hours of work will be thirty-five (35) hours each workweek; however, additional work will be necessary from time to time in order to fulfill the functions of your position, and it is understood that you will perform such work as necessary.

You will receive straight time pay for hours worked over thirty-five (35) and up to forty (40) in a given week, based on your regular hourly rate as specified below. You will also receive overtime pay for hours worked over forty (40) in a given week. The amount of overtime pay will be one and one-half times your regular hourly rate for all hours worked over forty (40).

This letter is intended only to set forth our understanding concerning your compensation and does not constitute an agreement as to the term of your employment. Either you or the (Employer) may terminate this employment relationship at any time and for any reason. In such a case, full compensation will be provided for all work actually performed on or before the next regular payday following termination.

It will be necessary under this system that you make an accurate record of your hours worked each workday and your total hours worked each workweek. Your fixed weekly salary, effective_____, 20___, will be _____, and your regular hourly rate based on your fixed salary will be $_____.

We request that you indicate your understanding and acceptance of this arrangement by countersigning this letter in the space indicated.

_____   _____
Employer   Employee

THIS DOCUMENT HAS BEEN PREPARED BY ICE MILLER ONLY TO SERVE AS A GUIDE IN DEVELOPING AN APPROPRIATE POLICY OR AGREEMENT. AN EMPLOYER SHOULD CONSULT WITH COUNSEL CONCERNING HOW THIS GUIDE SHOULD BE USED IN LIGHT OF ANY PARTICULAR FACTUAL SITUATION, AND TO DISCUSS CHANGES WHICH MAY HAVE OCCURRED IN THE UNDERLYING LAW AND REGULATIONS.

Although it is not common (and is not recommended) it is possible to establish that the fixed weekly salary includes compensation for gap time. In other words, an employee's fixed weekly salary is understood to include compensation for the normal fixed weekly hours and any work which may be required during the gap. (For obvious reasons, this arrangement is not popular with employees whose job requires work in gap!) As long as the arrangement is clearly established and understood by the employee, additional compensation for work from the fixed weekly hours up to 40 is not required (unless the regular hourly rate would otherwise be less than minimum wage), and overtime of time and one-half for the regular hourly rate for hours worked over 40 is required.

SAMPLE GAP TIME AGREEMENT (Non-Compensated)

This letter is intended to serve as a memo of our mutual understanding regarding compensation for your employment with _____. You will be employed as _____ at the _____ facility.

Effective _____, 20___, we will compensate you on the basis of a fixed weekly salary for up to forty (40) hours worked in each workweek. Your regular scheduled hours of work will be thirty-five (35) hours each workweek; however, additional work will be necessary from time to time in order to fulfill the functions of your position, and it is understood that you will perform such work as necessary. Your fixed weekly salary will cover up to five (5) hours of such additional work each week.

You will also receive overtime pay for hours worked over forty (40) in a given week. The amount of overtime pay will be one and one-half times your regular hourly rate for all hours worked over forty (40).

This letter is intended only to set forth our understanding concerning your compensation and does not constitute an agreement as to the term of your employment. Either you or the (Employer) may terminate this employment relationship at any time and for any reason. In such a case, full compensation will be provided for all work actually performed on or before the next regular payday following termination.

It will be necessary under this system that you make an accurate record of your hours worked each workday and your total hours worked each workweek. Your fixed weekly salary, effective _____, 20___, will be _____, and your regular hourly rate based on your fixed weekly salary will be $_____.

We request that you indicate your understanding and acceptance of this arrangement by countersigning this letter in the space indicated.

_____   _____
Employer   Employee

THIS DOCUMENT HAS BEEN PREPARED BY ICE MILLER ONLY TO SERVE AS A GUIDE IN DEVELOPING AN APPROPRIATE POLICY OR AGREEMENT. AN EMPLOYER SHOULD CONSULT WITH COUNSEL CONCERNING HOW THIS GUIDE SHOULD BE USED IN LIGHT OF ANY PARTICULAR FACTUAL SITUATION, AND TO DISCUSS CHANGES WHICH MAY HAVE OCCURRED IN THE UNDERLYING LAW AND REGULATIONS.

The fixed weekly hours under the fixed salary for fixed weekly hours arrangement may exceed 40 hours per week. In this case, half-time the regular hourly rate is required for hours worked from 40 up to the fixed weekly hours, and time and one-half for hours worked above the fixed weekly hours. Because the fixed weekly wage covers the straight time portion of hours worked up to the fixed weekly hours, only half-time is required to bring the employee's compensation up to time and one-half for those hours.

Fixed Salary for Fluctuating Hours

It is also possible to establish by clear cut agreement or understanding that a fixed salary will constitute compensation for all hours worked in the established workweek, *i.e.* the fixed salary will be compensation for fluctuating hours. In this case, there is no fixed regular rate, since the regular rate will vary each week depending on the number of hours worked. Because the fixed salary constitutes straight time compensation for all hours worked (and subject to the condition that the resulting average hourly rate always exceeds the minimum wage), overtime is only required at one-half the regular hourly rate for any hours worked over 40. The fixed salary constitutes straight time for all hours worked, including hours worked over 40, and the additional half-time premium brings an employee's compensation to the required time and one-half for hours worked over 40 under this arrangement.

This arrangement is expressly authorized by regulations of the Department of Labor; however, those regulations require that the employee affected have an "understanding with his employer that he will receive such fixed amount as straight time pay for whatever hours he is called upon to work in a workweek, whether few or many." It is essential that a written policy or understanding be established if the "fixed salary for fluctuating hours" overtime plan is to be used.

SAMPLE FIXED SALARY FOR
FLUCTUATING HOURS OVERTIME AGREEMENT

This letter is intended to serve as a memo of our mutual understanding regarding compensation for your employment with _____. You will be employed as _____ at the _____ facility.

Effective _____, 20___, we will compensate you on the basis of a fixed weekly salary for all hours worked in each workweek. This fixed salary will constitute your entire straight time compensation for the week, regardless of the number of hours actually worked. In this regard, your weekly salary will not be reduced for weeks in which you work, but work less than the full schedule of hours.

In addition to your fixed weekly salary, you will receive overtime pay for hours worked over forty (40) in a given week. The amount of overtime pay will equal one-half times your regular hourly rate for the week involved for all hours worked over forty (40). You should understand that your regular hourly rate will vary from week to week, depending on the total number of hours actually worked.

This letter is intended only to set forth our understanding concerning your compensation. It does not constitute an agreement as to the term of your employment. Either you or the (Employer) may terminate this employment relationship at any time and for any reason. In such a case, final compensation will be provided for all work actually performed on or before the next regular pay date following termination.

It will be necessary under this system that you make an accurate record of your hours worked each workday and your total hours worked each workweek. Your fixed weekly salary, effective _____ 20___, will be _____. We request that you indicate your understanding and acceptance of this arrangement by countersigning this letter in the space indicated.

_____   _____
Employer   Employee

There is a large downside to this plan. Because the employee's salary must constitute the employee's compensation for all hours worked (however many or however few), the employee must receive the full fixed salary even if the employee works less than expected or is absent for any reason. This limitation on deductions clearly makes the fixed salary for fluctuating hours plan inappropriate for employees prone to absenteeism.

Use of Fixed Salary Method to Resolve Back Pay for Individuals Denied Exempt Status

When the exemption status of an employee is challenged through a wage and hour audit or lawsuit, it is manifestly in the employer's interest to calculate any back overtime pay due on the basis of the fixed salary for fluctuating hours method. Only an additional half-time for hours worked over 40 is required for an individual whose exemption is denied, as long as the individual's salary was understood to compensate for all hours worked including overtime hours. Liability using this method is one-third what it would be using the time and one-half method.

Unfortunately, the records are often not clear concerning exactly what the salary was intended to cover. It is advisable to establish by policy or agreement that the salary paid to all exempt employees is intended to cover all hours worked, not just the employee's regular schedule. Use of this method to compute overtime back pay could be challenged if deductions from the fixed salary have been made for absences due to sickness, injury or for personal reasons, even though such deductions are permitted under the salary basis rules applicable to exempt personnel. However, the Department of Labor has typically permitted use of the fixed salary method to settle overtime back pay for individuals denied exempt status, unless it is clear that the salary was restricted to a fixed schedule of hours.

Salary Paid on Semi-Monthly Basis

If an employee is paid on a semi-monthly basis (*i.e.* twice per month, 24 pays per year), the semi-monthly salary must be converted to a weekly salary by multiplying the semi-monthly salary by 24 (the total semi-monthly periods during the year) and dividing by 52. Overtime must then be calculated based on hours worked over 40 in each established workweek (*i.e.* seven days, 168 hours). It is NOT permissible to calculate overtime by the "half month" or any other period longer than one established workweek. Any overtime pay earned would be paid on the next regular semi-monthly pay day, unless the calculation cannot reasonably be completed at that time. In other words, overtime is calculated by the week, and on any given pay day, an employee may receive overtime for the two or three workweeks which ended during the semi-monthly pay period.

If the semi-monthly salary covers the employee's entire straight time compensation for all hours worked, however many or however few, then the calculation of overtime is essentially the same as in the fixed salary for fluctuating hours method described above. The semi-monthly salary is again converted to a weekly salary, and overtime is calculated on a half-time basis for hours worked over 40 in each established workweek.

"Belo" Contracts – Guaranteed Weekly Pay Including Overtime

If an employee's duties necessitate irregular and fluctuating hours of work, and if the employer and employee enter into an express agreement (known as a "Belo" contract), which specifies a regular rate of pay, guaranteed weekly pay and weekly hours, not in excess of 60 hours per week, with compensation at not less than time and one-half the regular hourly rate for hours worked in excess of 40, then the employee will be permitted to receive a fixed weekly compensation including overtime that does not vary based on the number of hours worked, unless hours worked exceeds the weekly guarantee.

The key requirement for a valid Belo contract is that the employee's **duties** must necessitate irregular hours of work. Neither the employer nor employee can be able to control or anticipate the number of hours worked. Employees who may meet this requirement would include on-call servicemen, insurance adjustors and other whose work is dictated by the demands of customers, suppliers or other forces outside the employer's or the employee's control.

Also, the employee's hours must in fact fluctuate at least four hours from week to week, and the fluctuations must include both non-overtime and overtime hours; in other words, hours must vary below 40 and above 40 from week to week. The guaranteed rate and guaranteed hours must determine the total compensation received by the employee. Employees who earn regular bonuses or commissions cannot use the Belo contract. The hours need not fluctuate above the guaranteed weekly hours, but the guarantee cannot exceed 60 hours.

SAMPLE GUARANTEED WEEKLY PAY FOR FLUCTUATING HOURS (BELO CONTRACT)

<u>Caution</u>:   All of the requirements set forth below must be satisfied before this agreement will be placed into effect:

1.   The employee's duties must necessitate irregular and fluctuating hours of work. Such fluctuations must involve more than four hours from week to week, and must involve both overtime and non-overtime hours, *i.e.*, the employee's hours must fluctuate above and below forty in some weeks.

2.   The fluctuation in hours must not be at the discretion of the employee or the employer, but must be dictated by the nature of the work itself.

3.   The agreement must specify a regular hourly rate of pay (not less than the minimum wage).

4.   The agreement must specify compensation at not less than time and one-half the regular hourly rate for hours worked in excess of forty each week.

5.   The contract must specify a weekly guarantee of pay, which is on the basis of the regular hourly rate and overtime rate specified, but not to cover more than sixty hours.

6.   The employee's earnings must not regularly include any additional compensation in the form of regular bonuses, commissions, etc.

THIS DOCUMENT HAS BEEN PREPARED BY ICE MILLER ONLY TO SERVE AS A GUIDE IN DEVELOPING AN APPROPRIATE POLICY OR AGREEMENT. AN EMPLOYER SHOULD CONSULT WITH COUNSEL CONCERNING HOW THIS GUIDE SHOULD BE USED IN LIGHT OF ANY PARTICULAR FACTUAL SITUATION, AND TO DISCUSS CHANGES WHICH MAY HAVE OCCURRED IN THE UNDERLYING LAW AND REGULATIONS.

CONTRACT FORM

(Employer) hereby agrees to employ (Name of Employee) as (Name of Position) at a regular hourly rate of pay of $____ per hour for the first forty hours in any workweek and at the rate of $____ per hour for all hours worked in excess of forty in any workweek, with a guarantee that (Employee) will receive, in any week in which he performs any work for the employer, the sum of $_____ as total compensation, for all work performed up to and including sixty (60) hours in such workweek. For any hours in excess of sixty (60) in a workweek, you will receive time and one-half the regular hourly rate.

This letter is intended only to set forth our understanding concerning your compensation. It does not constitute an agreement as to the term of your employment. Either you or the (Employer) may terminate this employment relationship at any time and for any reason. In such a case, final compensation will be provided for all work actually performed on or before the next regular pay date following termination.

THIS DOCUMENT HAS BEEN PREPARED BY ICE MILLER ONLY TO SERVE AS A GUIDE IN DEVELOPING AN APPROPRIATE POLICY OR AGREEMENT. AN EMPLOYER SHOULD CONSULT WITH COUNSEL CONCERNING HOW THIS GUIDE SHOULD BE USED IN LIGHT OF ANY PARTICULAR FACTUAL SITUATION, AND TO DISCUSS CHANGES WHICH MAY HAVE OCCURRED IN THE UNDERLYING LAW AND REGULATIONS.

Belo contracts, although attractive because they provide a fixed compensation per week for non-exempt employees, are extremely limited in applicability and must be carefully reviewed to assure compliance with applicable regulations. If a Belo contract is found invalid, the employee is typically entitled to overtime back pay based on the fixed salary for fluctuating hours method.

Frequently Asked Questions about Calculation of Overtime

May employers average hours over two or more weeks?

No, employers may not average hours over two or more weeks in order to avoid paying overtime. For example, if an employee works 20 hours one week and 60 hours the next, he must receive overtime compensation for overtime hours worked beyond 40 in the second week, even though the average number of hours worked in both weeks is 40. The only exceptions, discussed above, are for hospitals, nursing homes and for public police and fire employees.

May an employer agree with the employee not to pay overtime, or refuse to pay overtime to an employee who works unauthorized overtime?

No, the overtime requirement may not be waived by agreement between the employer and employees. An agreement that only eight hours a day or only 40 hours a week will be counted as working time will not comply with the FLSA. In addition, an announcement by the employer that no overtime work will be permitted, or that overtime work will not be paid for unless authorized in advance, will not impair the employee's right to compensation for overtime hours that the employer suffers or permits to be worked, as described in Chapter 4. In other words, although an employer may discipline an employee who works unauthorized overtime hours, an employer may not refuse to pay overtime for those hours worked.

May an employer offer compensatory time off in lieu of paying overtime?

No, contrary to popular belief, PRIVATE sector employers may not provide employees with compensatory time off in lieu of paying overtime. PUBLIC sector employers, on the other hand, may reach an agreement or understanding with employees to permit compensatory time off up to a limit of 240 hours (480 for public safety employees). Legislation to extend compensatory time off for private sector employers has been debated in Congress, but has not been passed.

Chapter 7

Recordkeeping and Posting Requirements

Introduction

In addition to mandating compliance with the substantive provisions of wage and hour laws, both state and federal statutes require employers to create and maintain extensive records, to make those records available for inspection by appropriate authorities and to post certain notices to employees about their rights and the employer's obligations. The FLSA provides that every covered employer must make, keep and preserve certain records regarding wages, hours and other employment terms and conditions. The Act itself does not specifically define what records must be kept, in what form or for how long. Rather, the FLSA delegates responsibility for determining recordkeeping requirements to the Administrator of the Department of Labor's Wage and Hour Division. Regulations which spell out the recordkeeping requirements are summarized in this chapter; these and other federal wage and hour regulations can be accessed through the DOL website at www.dol.gov.

Several of the regulations deal with specific industries and classifications of employees that are allowed exceptions under the FLSA, and which are likely to be inapplicable to most readers (*e.g.*, country elevator employees, seamen and employees employed in certain tobacco, cotton, sugar cane or sugar beet services, to name a few). These industries and classifications are not specifically covered in this chapter; however, brief citations to these special industries and classifications are provided. This summary of the recordkeeping requirements is divided into two basic categories – information by the type or classification of employee (*e.g.*, non-exempt, exempt, agricultural, homeworker, etc.) and information by the type of payment practice (*e.g.*, tips, commissions, etc.). A discussion of retention and posting requirements follows.

General Requirements

Most state and federal wage and hour recordkeeping requirements are applicable to all employees. However, exempt employees and minors have special recordkeeping requirements.

Non-Exempt Employees

The core federal regulations require that employers keep the following information for all employees subject to the FLSA's minimum wage and overtime requirements (*e.g.*, non-exempt employees):

- name in full, as used for Social Security recordkeeping purposes, and on the same record, the employee's identifying symbol or number if such is used on any time, work or payroll records;

- home address, including zip code;

- date of birth, if under age 19. In satisfaction of this requirement, an employer may keep an age certificate, a work certificate or other proof of a minor's age;

- sex and occupation in which employed;

- time of day and day of week in which the employee's workweek begins (if the workweek for all employees is the same a single notation will suffice);

- regular hourly rate of pay for any workweek in which overtime compensation is due, including an explanation of the basis of the pay on a per hour, per day, per week, per piece, commission or other basis, if applicable, and the amount and nature of any payment excluded from the "regular rate;"

- hours worked for each workday and total hours worked for each workweek;

- total daily or weekly straight-time earnings or wages due for hours worked during the workday or workweek, exclusive of premium overtime compensation;

- total premium pay for overtime hours;

- total additions to or deductions from wages paid each pay period, including employee purchase orders or wage assignments and the dates, amounts and nature of the items that make up the total additions and deductions;

- total wages paid each pay period; and

- date of pay period and the pay period covered by payment.

If retroactive payments for wages are required and supervised by the DOL, certain other requirements apply.

Exempt Employees

With respect to persons employed in a bona fide executive, administrative or professional capacity, or as an Outside Salesperson (discussed in Chapter 3, above), employers need only maintain the records described in items 1 through 5, and 11 and 12, above. The employer must also record the basis upon which wages are paid, to permit calculation of the employee's total remuneration, including fringe benefits. Although, for exempt employees, employers are spared from meeting all of the recordkeeping requirements for their non-exempt counterparts, it is nonetheless important to keep in mind that there may be positions that are treated by the employer as exempt, but which may come under challenge from employees or the DOL as not truly meeting the criteria for exemption. In such cases, employers must be certain that they can produce records that prove that the exemption applies. Without records proving exemption and without records showing hours worked, an employer may not only end up paying a misclassified employee for all straight time and overtime worked, but may also have to rely on the employee's memory as how much time should be compensated.

Minors/Child Labor

Indiana law requires that employers keep for each minor employed, for a period of two years following termination of the employment relationship, a copy of the employment certificate, a copy of the termination notice if the minor left employment before the age of 18, a copy of the written parental permission as required for employment for certain activities and hours, and a copy of the Intention to Employ form provided to the issuing officer. The FLSA contains no special recordkeeping requirements for minors, except for students employed by virtue of special certificates at a sub-minimum wage, which is virtually obsolete in today's economy.

In addition to the above, employers must, of course, still keep and maintain for minor employees all of the normal records required under the FLSA for regular non-exempt and/or exempt employees, and for other classifications of employees and payment methods, as set forth below.

Special Requirements for Certain Classifications of Employees

Some industries and types of employees merit special recordkeeping requirements under the FLSA. Although not all of the special industries and employees addressed by the FLSA and the DOL are given attention in this chapter, a brief citation to other special classifications is provided in Section 7.

Agricultural Employees

Agricultural employers are spared from keeping any wage and hour records if they did not use more than 500 man-days of agricultural labor in any quarter of the preceding calendar year (unless it can be reasonably anticipated that at least 500 man-days will be used in at least one quarter of the current calendar year) and if they did not employ minors (except for their own children) on school days or in hazardous occupations. (A "man-day" is any day during which an employee does agricultural work of one hour or more. This term does not include days of work performed by members of the employer's immediate family.)

Agricultural employers who reasonably anticipate using more than 500 man-days of labor as set forth above must keep and maintain the following information for each employee:

- Name in full.

- Home address.

- Sex and occupation in which employed.

- Symbols or other identifications separately designating those employees who are members of the employer's immediate family, hand harvest laborers and employees principally engaged in the range production of livestock.

- For each employee not a member of the employer's immediate family, the number of man-days worked each week or each month.

For the entire year following a year in which the employer used more than 500 man-days of labor, the employer must keep all of the information required for non-exempt employees, except date of birth and total daily or weekly straight-time earnings or wages due for hours worked during the workday or workweek. Such employers must also keep a statement from each "hand harvest laborer" specifying the number of weeks employed in agriculture in the preceding year and, if the hand harvest laborer is 16 years of age or under and meets other exemption requirements, the minor's date of birth and name or parent of person standing in place of the parent.

Every agricultural employer (other than parents employing their own children) who employs any minor under age 18 on school days or in a hazardous occupation must also maintain and preserve records of the following with respect to each such minor:

- Name in full

- Place where minor lives while employed

- Date of birth

Industrial Homeworkers

Industrial homeworkers are persons allowed to produce goods for the employer from their home. In addition to all of the other records required for other employees (see Section B above), every employer of homeworkers must also record:

- Date on which the work was given to the worker, or begun by the worker, and the amount of such work given or begun

- Date on which the work was turned in by the worker and the amount of such work

- Kind of articles worked on and the operations performed

- Piece rates paid

- Hours worked on each lot turned in

- Name and address of any agent, distributor or contractor through whom the homework is distributed or collected and the name and address of each homeworker to who homework is distributed or from whom it is collected by each such agent, distributor or contractor

In addition to the records kept by the employer, each homeworker must keep a homeworker handbook, in which the employee tracks hours worked and other information used to compute wages owed. This handbook is shown to the employer at the end of the pay period, and the employer must certify that it has accurately recorded the contents. Once full, or upon the employee's termination, the employer must obtain and retain the handbook for a period of two years. Homeworker handbooks (Department of Labor Form WH-75) are available in several different languages from the Department of Labor's Wage and Hour Division (the office in Indiana is located in the Federal Building, 46 East Ohio Street, Room 413, Indianapolis, Indiana 46204; 317-226-6801).

Employees of Hospitals and Residential Care Facilities Compensated for Overtime Work on the Basis of a 14-Day Work Period

Under section 7(j) of the FLSA, employers operating hospitals and certain other healthcare facilities may agree with certain employees to calculate overtime on a 14-day instead of a seven day period, if the employer pays overtime compensation for hours worked over 80 in the 14-day period <u>and</u> for hours worked over eight in a day, as discussed in Chapter 6. In addition to the recordkeeping requirements imposed for other employees, employers utilizing the 14-day system must keep the following records, which primarily substitute the 14-day requirements for the generally applicable "workweek" requirements:

- Time of day and day of the week on which the employee's 14-day work period begins (instead of the "workweek" as for all other employees).

- Hours worked each workday and total hours worked each 14-day work period (instead of hours worked each workday and "workweek").

- Total straight-time wages paid for hours worked during the 14-day work period (instead of "weekly" straight-time wages).

- Total overtime excess compensation paid for hours worked in excess of eight in a workday and 80 in the work period (instead of over 40 in a "workweek").

In addition, the employer must keep a copy of the agreement and understanding with the employee with respect to the utilization of the 14-day period for overtime compensation, or a memorandum summarizing the terms of that agreement, the date it was entered into and how long it remains in effect if the agreement was not in writing.

Other Special Classifications of Employers or Employees

As mentioned above, the FLSA imposes special recordkeeping requirements on a number of other classes of employees and employers, most of which are not likely apply to the vast majority of employers. However, an employer that employs a person who may be classified in one of the following categories should consult the cited regulations or seek legal counsel to assist with the recordkeeping requirements:

- Livestock auction employees exempt from overtime pay requirements (29 C.F.R. § 516.13).

- Country elevator employees exempt from overtime pay requirements (29 C.F.R. § 516.14).

- Local delivery employees exempt from overtime pay requirements (29 C.F.R. § 516.15).

- Seamen exempt from overtime pay requirements (29 C.F.R. § 516.17).

- Employees employed in certain tobacco, cotton, sugar cane or sugar beet services exempt from overtime pay requirements (29 C.F.R. § 516.18).

- Employees employed under certain collective bargaining agreements who are partially exempt from overtime pay requirements (29 C.F.R. § 516.20).

- Bulk petroleum employees partially exempt from overtime pay requirements (29 C.F.R. § 516.21).

- Employees engaged in charter activities for a street, suburban or interurban electric railway or local trolley or motorbus carrier (29 C.F.R. § 516.22).

- Employees paid for overtime on the basis of two or more different hourly rates (29 C.F.R. § 516.25).

- Employees paid for overtime at premium rates computed on a "basic" rate authorized as being substantially equivalent to the average hourly earnings of the employee (29 C.F.R. § 516.26).

- Employees employed by a private entity operating an amusement or recreational establishment located in a national park or national forest or on land in the National Wildlife Refuge System who are partially exempt from overtime pay requirements (29 C.F.R. § 516.29).

Special Requirements for Alternative Payment Practices

In addition to employing special classes of employees, many employers also utilize special payment practices that go beyond the usual and customary methods of an hourly wage and overtime compensation system. These special payment practices are covered below.

Tips

Employers who include tips as a part of an employee's wages (discussed in Chapter 6) must record, in addition to the other information ordinarily required:

- A symbol, letter or other notation placed on the pay records identifying each employee whose wage is determined in part by tips.

- The weekly or monthly amount reported by the employee, to the employer, of tips received.

- The amount by which the wages of each tipped employee have been deemed to be increased by tips as determined by the employer (not in excess of 40 percent of the applicable statutory minimum wage).

- The hours worked each workday in any occupation in which the employee does not receive tips, and total daily or weekly straight-time payment made by the employer for such hours

- The hours worked each workday in occupations in which the employee receives tips, and total daily or weekly straight-time earnings for such hours.

Commissions

Retail or service establishments may employ commissioned employees who are exempt from overtime pay requirements if certain conditions are met (discussed in Chapter 3). In exchange, such employers must keep the following additional records:

- A symbol, letter or other notation placed on the payroll records identifying each employee who is so paid.

- A copy of the agreement or understanding under which this payment method is utilized or, if such agreement or understanding is not in writing, a memorandum summarizing its terms including the basis of compensation, the applicable representative period and the date the agreement was entered into and how long it remains in effect.

- Total compensation paid to each employee each pay period (showing separately the amount of commissions and the amount of non-commission straight-time earnings).

"Belo" Contracts

Some employees whose work necessitates irregular hours beyond the control of the employee or employer, may enter into special agreements with their employer to receive a flat payment to cover straight time and overtime compensation for those hours worked, referred to as a "Belo Contract," discussed in Chapter 6. Employers utilizing such a compensation system must keep all records and information ordinarily required for other employees, except for straight-time earnings and premium pay for overtime hours, which are inapplicable in the context of a Belo plan. In addition, they must keep the following information:

- Total weekly guaranteed earnings.

- Total weekly compensation in excess of the weekly guarantee.

- A copy of the individual contract or agreement, or where such contract or agreement is not in writing, a written memorandum summarizing its terms.

Non-Monetary Wages (Board and Lodging and Use of Other Facilities)

Employers who provide board, lodging and other facilities to employees may be able to count such items as wages, subject to certain qualifications and limitations (discussed in Chapter 5). Employers who utilize such facilities as a form of payment must maintain and preserve records substantiating the cost of furnishing such items.

Piece Work

Employers that pay employees for hours worked on the basis of a piece rate must maintain and preserve all of the records ordinarily required for other employees. Overtime compensation for piece workers is discussed at Chapter 6. In addition to the regular recordkeeping requirements, employers of piece workers must also keep the following records:

- Each piece rate at which the employee is employed

- The basis on which wages are paid

- The amount and nature of each payment that is excluded from the "regular rate"

- The number of units of work performed in the workweek at each applicable piece rate during any overtime hours

- The total weekly overtime compensation at each applicable piece rate that is over and above all straight-time earnings or wages earned during overtime worked

- The date of the agreement or understanding to use this method of compensation and the period covered

Retention and Inspection Requirements

In addition to creating the records discussed above, federal law also requires that employers maintain and preserve records for a period of either two or three years, and to make the records available for inspection and transcription by the DOL and its representatives. The records are to be kept at the place of employment or at one or more established central recordkeeping offices where such records are customarily maintained. When the records are kept at such a central location, the employer will be allowed 72 hours following notice to produce the records for inspection.

Records do not have to be preserved in their original, bulky form. The use of microfilm is an accepted method of preservation and retention if adequate viewing facilities are available. The duplicated records should not be destroyed before making sure that the reproductions clearly and accurately reflect the original records, that they are identifiable as to dates and pay periods, and that they are in chronological order.

The regulations also provide that an employer may petition the Department of Labor for authority to maintain records in a manner other than those specified by the regulations or to be relieved of preserving certain records. Such authority may be granted under specified conditions.

Federal law makes it unlawful for an employer to violate the recordkeeping requirements and to knowingly falsify records or reports. The FLSA imposes civil and in some cases criminal penalties for such violations. The FLSA also sanctions civil actions to enjoin violations of the recordkeeping requirements.

Employers must preserve the following records (which are described in detail above) for at least three years:

- Payroll records.

- Sales and purchase records relating to volume of sales and business and goods purchased and received.

- Certificates, agreements, plans, notices, etc., such as:

    - Agreements relied upon for provision of board, lodging, or other facilities as part of wages.

    - Plans, trusts, employment contracts and collective bargaining agreements relating to exemptions or exclusions from the calculation of the regular rate of pay.

    - Individual Belo contracts or agreements (fixed wages for fluctuating hours).

    - Agreements relating to piece work, multiple hourly rates and any change in the workweek to a 14-day pay period.

    - All certificates and notices listed or named in any applicable part of the regulations.

Each employer must also keep the following "supplementary basic records" (basically, the source documents for all other records) for a period of two years:

- Basic employment and earnings records – these materials would include time cards or records showing production (in the case of piece rates) and records showing earnings

- Wage rate tables – these would be tables that show the rates used to calculate straight earnings, wages, salary or overtime

- Order, shipping, and billing records – these records would include all customer orders or invoices received, incoming or outgoing shipping or delivery records, as well as all bills of lading and all billings to customers (not including individual sales slips, cash register tapes and the like) which the employer retains or makes in the usual course of business operations

- Records of additions to or deductions from wages paid

Posting Requirements

Both state and federal laws require that employers post in a conspicuous place where their employees work certain information regarding employees' rights and employer's obligations under state and federal wage and hour laws. The appropriate state and federal agencies have prepared and will readily make available, upon request, posters covering each of these requirements. The state and federal posting requirements (listed by the title of the poster) are as follows:

Federal Postings

- Equal Employment Opportunity is the Law

- Your Rights Under the Fair Labor Standards Act;

- Notice – Employee Polygraph Protection Act

- Your Rights Under the Family and Medical Leave Act

- Job Safety and Health Protection

If an employer is working on a federally funded project, the employer may also be required to post the Notice to Employees Working on Federal or Federal Financed Construction Projects poster or a Notice to Employees Working on Government Contracts poster. Additional posting requirements may also apply.

Indiana Postings

- Indiana Minimum Wage Law

- Notice of Teen Worker Hour Restrictions

- Indiana Employment and Training Services Act

- Indiana Worker's Compensation Notice

- Equal Opportunity is the Law

- Safety and Health Protection on the Job

Chapter 8
Child Labor Provisions

Overview

The federal government, through the Fair Labor Standards Act (FLSA), and the state of Indiana have implemented child labor laws and regulations designed to protect the educational opportunities of minors and prohibit their employment in jobs under conditions detrimental to their health or well-being. The FLSA and Indiana law set out specific requirements for the employment of minors, including restrictions on the nature of the work performed and limitations on the hours worked by minors. The rules vary with the age of the minor worker and the occupation. At age 18, a worker is not covered by the child labor provisions of either the FLSA or Indiana law and may work an unlimited number of hours in any occupation.

Not all child labor is unlawful. In fact, with the exceptions listed below, the FLSA and Indiana law permit the employment of minors beginning at the age of 14. Some jobs held by youths, such as delivering newspapers and performing in motion pictures and theatrical, radio and television productions, are specifically exempted from FLSA and Indiana child labor provisions and may be performed by minors under age 14.

What the federal and state child labor laws seek to prohibit is oppressive child labor that interferes with the health and well-being of the child. What constitutes unlawful child labor varies with such factors as the age of the child, the industry, the nature of the occupation, parental involvement, conflicts with schooling and other considerations of a minor's health and well-being. Accordingly, employment of a minor in a given industry, occupation or set of circumstances may be considered unlawful in one industry, occupation or set of circumstances, but not in another.

Employers may be subject to either the FLSA, or the Indiana child labor provisions or both. When the FLSA and Indiana child labor provisions are applicable, the law with the more stringent standard must be obeyed.

These materials will address the child labor laws within the context of the requirements under the FLSA and will note exceptions under Indiana law.

Coverage

The FLSA applies to employees and employers involved in interstate commerce, as discussed in Chapter 2. Indiana's child labor provisions generally apply to all employers doing business in Indiana regardless of their size or number of employees. However, a parent or guardian who employs their own child is exempt from Indiana's child labor provisions, except those provisions concerning underage employment, employment during school hours and employment in hazardous occupations designated by federal law.

Nonagricultural Employment

Minimum Age and Hours of Work

The child labor provisions of the FLSA establish both hours and occupational standards for minors. Children of any age are generally permitted to work for a business owned entirely by their parents, except those under 16 may not be employed in mining or manufacturing, and no one under 18 may be employed in any occupation the Secretary of Labor has declared to be hazardous. The FLSA places the following restrictions on the employment of minors:

- **Eighteen-year-olds and up.** Once a youth reaches the age of 18, he or she is no longer subject to the FLSA and may be employed for unlimited hours in any occupation.

- **Sixteen and 17-year-olds.** Under the FLSA, minors in this category may work unlimited hours and any nonhazardous job. Section 2 explains what is considered hazardous for this purpose. Indiana law does restrict the hours, times and days that 16 and 17-years olds may work, discussed in Section 4.

- **Fourteen and 15-year-olds.** The FLSA imposes a number of restrictions on this age group with respect to the hours and jobs they may work.

- **Hours worked:** Fourteen and 15 year-olds are limited to working the following hours:

  - Outside school hours

  - No more than three hours on a school day

  - No more than eight hours on a non-school day

  - No more than 18 hours during a week when school is in session

  - Between 7:00 a.m. and 7:00 p.m.—except between June 1 and Labor Day when the evening hour is extended to 9:00 p.m. (But note, Indiana law restricts 14 and 15 year olds from working before 7:30 a.m. discussed below.)

School hours are determined by the local public school in the area the minor is residing while employed. This is true even if the minor does not attend the public school (*i.e.*, attends a private school or is home schooled).

Prohibited occupations: Minors aged 14 and 15 may not work in the following occupations:

- Any manufacturing occupation

- Any mining occupation

- Processing occupations such as filleting of fish, dressing poultry, cracking nuts or laundering as performed by commercial laundries and dry cleaning (except in a retail, food service or gasoline service establishment, and under the restrictions provided for those establishments)

- Occupations requiring the performance of any duties in workrooms or workplaces where goods are manufactured, mined or otherwise processed (except in a retail, food service or gasoline service establishment, and under the restrictions provided for those establishments)

- Public messenger service

- Operation or tending of hoisting apparatus or of any power-driven machinery (other than office machines and certain machines in retail, food service or gasoline service establishments, and under the restrictions provided for those establishments)

- Any occupations found and declared to be hazardous

- Occupations in connection with:

  - Transportation of persons or property by rail, highway, air, on water, pipeline or other means

  - Warehousing and storage

  - Communications and public utilities

  - Construction, including repair (except office or sales work in connection with these occupations when not performed on transportation media or at the actual construction site)

- Any of the following occupations in a retail, food service or gasoline service establishment:

  - Work performed in or about boiler or engine rooms

  - Work in connection with maintenance or repair of the establishment, machines or equipment

  - Outside window washing that involves working from window sills, and all work requiring the use of ladders, scaffolds or their substitutes

  - Cooking (except at soda fountains, lunch counters, snack bars or cafeteria serving counters) and baking

  - Occupations which involve operating, setting up, adjusting, cleaning, oiling or repairing power-driven food slicers and grinders, food choppers and cutters, and bakery-type mixers

  - Work in freezers and meat coolers in preparation of meats for sale (except wrapping, sealing, labeling, weighing, pricing and stocking when performed in other areas)

  - Loading and unloading goods to and from trucks, railroad cars or conveyors, and

  - All occupations in warehouses (except office and clerical work)

Permitted employment: Except for the prohibitions listed above, 14 and 15-year-olds may be employed in occupations in retail, food service, grocery stores and gasoline service establishments and can perform a variety of jobs, such as:

- Bag and carry out customer orders
- Sell
- Model
- Do art work
- Clean fruits and vegetables
- Clean-up work and grounds maintenance (but not use power tools)
- Stock goods
- Prepare and serve food and drinks (but not cook or bake)
- Perform office or clerical work
- Deliver items by foot, bicycle or public transportation

Hazardous Employment

Federal law forbids the employment of minors in hazardous occupations prohibited under the child labor provisions of the FLSA. There are 17 hazardous non-agricultural jobs that are prohibited for young workers below the age of 18 as identified by the Secretary of Labor in various Hazardous Orders (H.O.) and listed in the Federal Register. These restrictions against hazardous employment constitute the centerpiece of the child labor restrictions; separate restrictions apply to agricultural occupations. The prohibited/hazardous occupations for minors under 18 are listed as the following:

- [H.O. 1] Manufacturing or storing explosives
- [H.O. 2] Driving a motor vehicle or work as an outside helper on motor vehicles
- [H.O. 3] Coal mining

- [H.O. 4] Logging and operating any sawmill, lathe mill, shingle mill or cooperage stock mill

- [H.O. 5] Operating power driven woodworking machines

- [H.O. 6] Occupations involving exposure to radioactive substances and to ionizing radiations

- [H.O. 7] Operating power-driven hoisting equipment

- [H.O. 8] Operating power-driven metal forming, punching and shearing machines

- [H.O. 9] Mining, other than coal

- [H.O. 10] Operating meat packing or processing, including power-driven meat slicing machines and retail and food service establishments

- [H.O. 11] Operating power-driven bakery machines, including mixers

- [H.O. 12] Operating power-driven paper products machines, including balers and compactors

- [H.O. 13] Manufacturing brick, tile and related products

- [H.O. 14] Operating power-driven circular saws, band saws and guillotine shears

- [H.O. 15] Wrecking, demolition and ship breaking operations

- [H.O. 16] Roofing operations

- [H.O. 17] Excavation operations

The regulations provide a limited exemption from H.O.s 5, 8, 10, 12, 14, 16 and 17 for apprentices and student learners who are at least 16 years of age and enrolled in approved programs. The term "operation" as used in H.O.s 5, 8, 10, 11, 12 and 14 generally includes the tasks of operating, setting up, adjusting, repairing, oiling or cleaning the equipment.

Restrictions on teenage driving. Public law 105-334, which became effective on October 31, 1988, amends the FLSA to modify H.O.2. That provision prohibits minors under 18 years old to drive on public roadways as part of their employment. However, 17-year-olds may drive for their employers on public roadways, but only if all the following conditions are met:

- Such driving is restricted to daylight hours

- The minor holds a state driver's license valid for the type of driving involved in the job

- The minor has successfully completed a state-approved driver education course

- The automobile or truck is equipped with a seat belt for the driver and any passengers and the employer has instructed the minor that the seat belts must be used when driving the automobile or truck

- The automobile or truck does not exceed 6,000 pounds of gross vehicle weight; such driving does not include:

  - the towing of vehicles

  - route deliveries or route sales

  - the transportation for hire of property, goods or passengers

  - urgent, time-sensitive deliveries

  - more than two trips away from the primary place of employment in any single day for the purpose of delivering goods of the minor's employer or to a customer (other than urgent, time-sensitive deliveries)

  - more than two trips away from the primary place of employment in any single day for the purpose of transporting passengers (other than employees of the employer)

  - transporting more than three passengers (including employees of the employer)

  - driving beyond a 30-mile radius from the minor's place of employment, and

  - such driving is only occasional and incidental to the minor's employment

The term "occasional and incidental" means no more than one-third of a minor's worktime in any workday and no more than 20 percent of a minor's worktime in any workweek.

Statutory Exemptions

The FLSA sets 14 as the minimum age for most nonagricultural work. However, those younger can still deliver papers, work in show business, work in businesses owned by a parent or guardian (but not in manufacturing, mining or hazardous jobs), baby-sit, and do household chores.

Actors and performers. Federal regulations exempt from child labor prohibitions children of any age who are employed as actors or performers in motion pictures or theatrical, radio and television productions. The regulations broadly define "performer" to include singers, dancers, musicians, comedians or anyone who affords amusement to a radio or television audience.

Newspaper delivery. Children who are engaged in delivering newspapers to consumers are exempt from the FLSA's child labor provisions. This exemption covers children who deliver newspapers to subscribers' homes, to newspaper consumers or who sell newspapers on the street. Also exempted are children who deliver shopping circulars and other advertising materials that are inserted into newspapers.

Parental employment. As noted above, children of any age are generally permitted to work for businesses owned entirely by their parents, except those under 16 may not be employed in mining or manufacturing, and no one under 18 may be employed in any occupation the Secretary of Labor has declared to be hazardous. The parental exemption applies only where the child is exclusively employed by the parent or guardian, not when the child is dually employed by the parent and another person. Thus, the exemption is not available if the child works for a corporation, even if the parent owns substantially all its stock and is an active manager.

Indiana Child Labor Provisions

Indiana law prohibits the employment of minors in occupations prohibited under the child labor provisions of the FLSA (discussed above). However, Indiana's child labor provisions impose additional restrictions to those contained in the FLSA regarding the employment of minors, including the number of hours per day and per week that minors under the age of 18 may work, and the issuance of work permits to minors. The Indiana provisions apply to minors employed in nonagricultural and agricultural occupations.

Fourteen and 15-year-olds. The restrictions with respect to the number of hours 14 and 15 year-olds may work per day and per week and the prohibited occupations for youth in this group are the same under the FLSA and Indiana law. However, it is important for employers to note that, unlike the FLSA, Indiana law specifically defines school hours as being between 7:30 a.m. and 3:30 p.m. Except for the exemptions discussed below, all minors are restricted from working those hours on days when school is in session.

Sixteen and 17-year-olds. Unlike the FLSA, Indiana law places a number of restrictions on the hours, times, and days that 16 and 17-year-olds may work. Specifically, Indiana law restricts the hours that minors in that group may work to the following:

- Outside the hours of 7:30 a.m. and 3:30 p.m. on school days

- No more than eight hours on a school day

- No more than 30 hours during a week when school is in session

- No more than 40 hours a week when school is not in session

- Between the hours of 6:00 a.m. and 10:00 p.m. on school days

- Between the hours of 6:00 a.m. and 10:00 p.m. on non-school days (16-year-olds only)

For the purposes of Indiana's child labor laws, a non-school week is defined as a week that contains two or fewer school days. A school day refers to a day that contains more than four hours of classroom instruction. A school week refers to a week that contains three or more school days.

Exception to hours restriction. Indiana law allows for 16 and 17-year-olds to work extended hours with written permission from a parent or guardian. With written permission, 16 and 17-year-olds may work up to 40 hours a week when school is in session and up to 48 hours per week when school is not in session. Additionally, 16 year-olds may work until midnight on days not followed by a school day with written parental permission. Seventeen-year-olds may work until 1:00 a.m. on no more than two non-consecutive nights followed by a school day, and until 11:30 p.m. on the remainder of the nights with written parental permission. In addition, 16 and 17-year-olds may work between 7:30 a.m. and 3:30 p.m. on a school day with written permission issued by the school that the minor attends.

Finally, minors aged 16 or 17 that have graduated from high school or have received a General Educational Development (GED) diploma are not subject to the hour restrictions and not required to obtain a work permit. Also, 16 and 17-year-olds that have withdrawn from school are not subject to the hour restrictions, but are required to obtain a work permit.

Teen Break Law. Most Indiana employers must provide one or two breaks totaling 30 minutes to minors under the age of 18 who are scheduled to work six or more consecutive hours. The law exempts for this requirement: farm laborers, domestic service workers, golf caddies, newspaper carriers, minors that have completed an approved vocational or special education program and minors that have withdrawn from school.

Agricultural Employment

Minimum Age and Hours of Employment

The hours and jobs minors may perform in agricultural jobs are slightly different than in nonagricultural occupations. Specifically, under the FLSA, minors of any age may be employed at any time in any occupations in agriculture on a farm owned or operated by their parent or guardian. However, the FLSA places restrictions on minors who work on farms not owned by a parent or guardian. As with nonagricultural jobs, the FLSA's restrictions depend on the age of the worker and the kind of job performed.

Sixteen-year-olds and above. The minors in this group can work on any day, for any number of hours and in any job in agriculture.

Fourteen and 15-year-olds. They may work on any farm, but only during hours when school is not in session and only in nonhazardous jobs.

Twelve and 13-year-olds. The FLSA provides that 12 and 13-year-olds may only work in agriculture, on a farm, if a parent has given written permission, or a parent is working on the same farm. The work can only be performed during hours when school is not in session and in non-hazardous jobs.

Eleven-year-olds and under. These young workers can only work in agriculture, on a farm, if the farm is not required to pay the federal minimum wage.

Hazardous Employment

As directed by the FLSA, the Secretary of Labor has found and declared certain agricultural tasks to be particularly hazardous for employees under the age of 16. Minors under 16 may not work in the following occupations:

- operating a tractor of over 20 PTO horsepower, or connecting or disconnecting an implement or any of its parts to or from such a tractor

- operating or working with a corn picker, cotton picker, grain combine, hay mower, forage harvester, hay baler, potato digger, mobile pea viner, feed grinder, crop dryer, forage blower, auger conveyor, unloading mechanism of a nongravity-type self-unloading wagon or trailer, power post-hole digger, power post driver or nonwalking-type rotary tiller

- operating or working with a trencher or earthmoving equipment, forklift, potato combine, or power-driven circular, band or chain saw

- working in a yard, pen or stall occupied by a bull, boar or stud horse maintained for breeding purposes; a sow with suckling pigs; or a cow with a newborn calf (with umbilical cord present)

- felling, bucking, skidding, loading or unloading timber with a butt diameter of more than six inches

- working from a ladder or scaffold at a height of over 20 feet

- driving a bus, truck or automobile to transport passenger(s), or riding on a tractor as a passenger or helper

- working inside: a fruit, forage, or grain storage designed to retain an oxygen-deficient or toxic atmosphere; an upright silo within two weeks after silage has been added or when a top unloading device is in operating position; a manure pit; or a horizontal silo while operating a tractor for packing purposes

- handling or applying toxic agricultural chemical(s) identified by the words "danger," "poison," or "warning" or a skull and crossbones on the label

- handling or using explosives

- transporting, transferring or applying anhydrous ammonia

Statutory Exemptions

The FLSA's child labor provisions, including those regarding hazardous occupations, do not apply to those youth employed on a family farm (commonly referred to as the "family farm" exemption). The FLSA provides that youth of any age may be employed at any time, in any occupation, on a farm owned or operated by their parents or persons standing in place of the parent. Additional exemptions include:

- 14 and 15-year-old student learners enrolled in vocational agriculture programs are exempt from the first six agricultural hazardous occupations listed above when certain requirements are met; and

- minors aged 14 and 15 who hold certificates of completion of training under a 4-H or vocational agriculture training program may work outside school hours on equipment listed in the first two items above for which they have been trained.

Indiana Law for Agricultural Child Labor

The Indiana child labor provisions discussed above regarding the employment in nonagricultural occupations also apply to minors employed in agricultural jobs. Additionally, the family farm exemption under the FLSA does not apply to minors who reside in Indiana. Indiana law prohibits minors of all ages from being employed during school hours or in hazardous occupations, regardless of whether they are employed by a parent. Since Indiana law is more stringent than the FLSA in this respect, it applies.

Employment Certificates Required

Except in limited circumstances defined in law and summarized below, all minors less than 18 years of age employed in the state of Indiana must have an employment certificate (commonly referred to as a work permit) to work. The FLSA also requires a certificate of age for working minors. The state employment certificate is accepted as the federal certificate of age. The minor's school issues the employment certificate.

Employers must have each minor employee's employment certificate on file and available for inspection by labor officials at all times. Employment certificates are always required, even when school is not in session. Certificates are issued for specific employment at a specified address. Only one work permit can be issued to a minor at a time. An issuing officer may not issue a subsequent work permit until a termination notice has been received on the initial work permit or the issuing officer has otherwise determined that the minor's employment has been terminated.

Certificates may not be issued that violate any provision of law. Thus, all restrictions on minimum ages for employment in various occupations and all work hour restrictions must be strictly followed. Neither school nor labor officials are empowered to waive, at any time or under any circumstances, any minimum labor standard established by law or regulation.

Minors work with the permission of the local school district. Thus, a minor may be denied a certificate if his attendance is not in good standing with the school or if his academic performance does not meet the standards of the school corporation in which he resides. The denial of a work permit may be appealed to the principal of the school that the minor attends. The work permit may then be issued or denied at the discretion of the principal.

Work certificates may also be revoked at any time by the issuing officer or the Indiana Department of Labor, whenever the conditions for the issuance of the certificate or permit do not exist, no longer exist or have never existed. An issuing officer who revokes a work permit shall immediately send written notice of the revocation to the minor's employer. A minor whose work permit is revoked is entitled to a periodic review, to be conducted not less than once per school year, to determine whether the revocation should continue. If, upon review, the issuing officer determines that the conditions that resulted in the revocation of the work permit have improved substantially, the issuing officer may reissue a work permit to the minor.

Enforcement of Child Labor Provisions

Federal Law

The Wage and Hour Division of the United States Department of Labor administers and enforces the child labor provisions of the FLSA, as discussed in Chapter 8. Violators of the child labor provisions may be subject to a civil money penalty of up to $10,000 for each minor employed in violation of the FLSA.

The FLSA also prohibits the shipment in interstate commerce of goods that were produced in violation of the Act's child labor provisions. The FLSA authorizes the Department of Labor to obtain injunctions to prohibit the movement of such "hot goods." The FLSA's hot goods restriction applies to an entity that produces, manufactures, mines, handles, or in any other manner works on goods in any state. Moreover, it applies even where the underage employee does not engage in producing the goods if, somewhere in the establishment "in or about" where he or she is employed, goods are "produced" for shipment or delivery in commerce.

Indiana Law

The Wage and Hour Division of the Indiana Department of Labor administers and enforces the Indiana's child labor laws. The Wage and Hour Division has the authority to conduct investigations and gather data on wages, hours and other employment conditions or practices in order to determine compliance with Indiana's child labor laws. Under Indiana's child labor laws, warnings are issued and penalties are assessed for each violation. Any employer found violating Indiana's child labor laws may be assessed civil penalties by the Bureau of Child Labor in the following manner:

+ The employer will be issued a warning letter for the first violation.

+ If the employer is cited for a second time during the one-year period following the issuance of the initial warning letter, he/she will be assessed a penalty for a second violation. (If the second violation is cited more than one year after the issuance of the initial warning letter, the process begins anew and the employer will be issued a warning letter.)

+ If the employer is cited for an additional violation after a second violation has been cited, he/she will be assessed a penalty for a third violation. (If the third violation occurs more than two years after the second violation, the process begins anew and the employer will be issued a warning letter.)

◆ For each violation thereafter, the employer will be assessed a penalty for each subsequent violation. (If the subsequent violation occurs more than two years after the previous violation, the process begins anew and the employer will be issued a warning letter.)

Chapter 9

Enforcement of Wage and Hour Laws

Brief Overview of Structure of the Department of Labor

Department of Labor Generally

The enforcement of the Act is entrusted to the Department of Labor (DOL). At the top of the organization chart for the DOL is the office of the Secretary of Labor, who is empowered to delegate much of the administrative enforcement of the Act. Among the many administrative agencies that report to the Secretary of Labor is the Employment Standards Administration. In turn, among the many offices of the Employment Standards Administration is the Wage and Hour Division (WHD). The WHD administers the wage, hour and child labor provisions of the Act, as well as several other programs covering prevailing wages for government contracts and farm labor, Family and Medical Leave and immigration. Civil litigation is managed by the Office of the Solicitor and criminal prosecution under the Act is specifically assigned to the Attorney General.

Structure of the Wage and Hour Division

The WHD is currently composed of regional, district, area and field offices located throughout the United States. The midwest region currently includes more than a dozen offices located in Illinois, Iowa, Kansas, Michigan, Minnesota, Missouri, Nebraska, Ohio, Wisconsin and Indiana. The midwest regional office is located in Chicago, Illinois; however, there is also a district office located in Indianapolis and an area office located in South

Bend. There are also field offices located in New Albany, Evansville, Muncie, Fort Wayne, Gary and Wabash. The most current information regarding the structure, location and contact information for WHD offices can be located at the DOL website, www.dol.gov.

Investigations Under the FLSA

Authority of the Secretary of Labor Under the Act

Among the major laws enforced by the DOL are the Occupational Safety and Health Act, the Employee Retirement Income Security Act, the Uniformed Services Employment and Reemployment Rights Act, the Family and Medical Leave Act and the Fair Labor Standards Act. Section 11(a) of the Act grants broad authorization to the Secretary of Labor, or designated representatives, to investigate and gather information regarding violations of the Act. Section 11(a) also provides authorization to enter onto an employer's premises, inspect an employer's place of business, inspect an employer's records, question employees, investigate facts, conditions, practices or any other matters that are necessary to determine compliance or non-compliance with the Act.

Initiation of an Investigation

Generally, WHD determines which employers will be investigated by utilizing two different mechanisms:

- incoming complaints; and

- industry-based investigations (sometimes referred to as "directed investigations").

Complaints are usually filed by current employees, ex-employees or occasionally by an employer's competitors. The motivation for current or former employees to file complaints is obvious: they believe that their rights were violated and they desire a means to collect damages. Competitors have been known to file complaints based on a real or perceived belief that their competitor has obtained some unfair business advantage by violating the Act.

With respect to incoming complaints, whenever possible, WHD attempts to prioritize such complaints based on the seriousness of the alleged violation, rather than strictly on a first-come, first-served basis. Due to limited resources, priority is generally given to complaints that allege very significant or dangerous violations, such as child labor violations or allegations that involve a significant number of employees. WHD will also review the allegations to determine if the breadth of the alleged violation indicates that it should be given higher priority, such as allegations involving multi-state or nationwide employers. Finally, WHD is also very practical in its approach to prioritizing investigations in that it accesses the resources that will be necessary to investigate the alleged violation in view of the potential benefits that may be recovered if the investigation uncovers violations of the Act.

In an industry-based investigation, or WHD-directed investigation, it is a well-guarded secret as to how an employer is selected. Oftentimes it appears that an investigation is initiated based on a particular industry's history of violations or when there is a perceived and/or long-term problem. However, just as often, the WHD-directed investigation appears to be based on a random selection.

Access to Employer Records and Personnel

The Act specifically authorizes WHD investigators to review employer records and interview witnesses to obtain information concerning compliance with the Act. Among the first things an investigator usually does is to request to review a number of different categories of documents. The kinds of records generally requested are those that will reveal information about employee pay rates, overtime hours worked and recorded, other payroll records, records regarding bonus payments or other forms of compensation, documents showing deductions from employee pay and records such as job descriptions that could be used to substantiate the applicability of exemptions under the Act. Investigators also often like to review employee "time cards" or similar time tracking records and compare them to pay records to look for minimum wage and overtime violations. Investigators may also ask to review I-9 forms and Family and Medical Leave Act compliance documentation, such as posters and certification forms. These records are used for the purpose of determining not only compliance with recordkeeping requirements of the Act, but also to investigate compliance with the substantive provisions of the Act.

Under most circumstances, employer records should only be reviewed by the investigator on company property. The records cannot be removed without the employer's express consent. The investigator should not request to remove any employer records from company property, unless it is absolutely necessary in order to conduct the investigation. If the employer does consent to the removal of any records, a very detailed receipt should be prepared and the employer should request the investigator to sign a receipt specifically indicating every record that is taken.

Interviews

Initial Employer Interview

Usually, the WHD investigator will attempt to schedule a time with the employer's representative to discuss the complaint at the employer's place of business where the violation is alleged or believed to have occurred. However, this is not to say that a compliance officer will never show up unannounced. Much of the approach depends on the personality of the investigator, the history of the employer and the general relationship with the DOL office conducting the investigation. Upon his or her arrival, the investigator will generally present his or her official credentials and conduct what is usually referred to as an "opening conference." The opening conference consists of an interview with the employer's representative. The discussion centers on the nature and scope of the investigation. The main purpose of the opening conference is to gather background information to determine jurisdiction and get a general feel for the facility, the employees and general recordkeeping practices. The background information that will usually be requested includes: documentation to substantiate the official legal name of the business and its corporate structure; the identities and positions of certain company officials (some may be specific to the complaint and other may be of a more general nature); the addresses and telephone numbers of the company's headquarters and subsidiaries and affiliates, if any; information regarding jurisdictional matters (dollar volume of sales, number of employees, etc.); a description of, or documentation regarding, the employer's standard workweek, work day and shift work; a general description or documentation of when lunch breaks are provided to employees; a general description of pay practices; and a discussion of recordkeeping practices.

The WHD investigator may also request a tour of the facility so he or she can look at the area where the complaining party works or worked, attempt to observe compliance with posting requirements, personally observe potential child labor violations and the general type of work being performed in the facility. It is a common practice for many employers, especially manufacturing employers, to request visitors to sign in and execute a release of liability associated with any tour of the manufacturing area. While an employer can require a WHD investigator to sign a visitor's log or similar document, under no circumstances will he or she sign a release of liability associated with the visit. If an employer attempts to require such a release in connection with a facility tour, the investigator will likely treat it as a refusal to allow the investigator to enter onto the premises.

A refusal to permit a WHD investigator onto the premises in order to conduct an investigation is a very serious matter that must be considered fully. Consultation with legal advisors should be sought before refusing access. A refusal to allow an investigator onto the premises will usually result in the investigator becoming agitated. He or she will usually think the employer is attempting to hide something, which results in increased attention to the complaint. The investigator is then forced to seek a subpoena to gain access to the information being sought.

Employee Interviews

It is not uncommon for the WHD investigator to conduct interviews of employees to either verify information obtained from the employer representative or obtain additional information. The WHD investigator will generally be trying to determine the accuracy of records provided by the employer, attempting to prove violations and questioning employees about exemptions that might apply under the Act. It is important to bear in mind that there is a distinct difference between the interview of a management employee and a non-management employee. The WHD investigator will allow an employer representative and legal counsel to be present during any interview or questioning of a management employee; however, interviews with non-management personnel are conducted confidentially, outside the presence of any management representative. If an employer insists that the WHD investigator not conduct an interview with a non-management employee without an employer representative present, the investigator will consider this a refusal to cooperate with the investigation and simply schedule the interview with the employee after work hours. At that point, the investigator will have the employee come to the investigator's office. Then, the investigator will make a home visit or will conduct the interview by telephone. If possible, the employer should allow the interview of non-management employee on company premises.

During the course of an interview with a non-management employee, the WHD investigator will likely take very detailed notes or take down the witness' statement on a computer (investigators do not generally record audio versions of interviews, and never without the consent of the person being interviewed). Much as is the case with other federal agency investigations, the statements are maintained as strictly confidential and will not be divulged to the employer, unless and until the employee testifies at a hearing in which the statement and/or testimony is used. Only at that point will the employer be given access to the statement for purposes of cross-examination.

Final Conference/Interview

After the WHD investigator has concluded the investigation, the investigator will generally meet with the employer representative for a final conference. The investigator will notify the employer representative of any violations that were determined to exist. The final conference is followed by an attempt by the WHD to resolve the matter without litigation.

Expedited Investigation

In addition to the process of conducting full investigations, the WHD occasionally uses a process referred to as "expedited investigation." In essence, the expedited investigation consists of the WHD requesting the employer to conduct an internal "self-audit" by reviewing its own records, policies and practices to determine if a violation has taken place. Oftentimes, the WHD investigator will ask for the employer's supporting records and documentation to verify that the employer is being forthcoming with regard to its self-audit. This process can be a very efficient method for the WHD to clear its docket of complaints of a low level of priority and also a cost-effective way for employers to avoid full-blown investigations.

Settlements and Conciliations

In the event that the WHD determines through its investigative process that an employer has violated the Act, the employer will usually be presented with the opportunity to settle or conciliate the complaint. The employer will be asked to "make whole" any employees who have lost pay as a result of the unlawful practice, by way of back wages. These amounts are often negotiable, especially if the alleged violation is not clear and unmistakable. In addition, the WHD will ask the employer for its commitment to comply with the Act. It often makes sense for employers to settle complaints, especially if the violation is clear. In the event that the employer is able and willing to resolve a complaint, without litigating the matter in court, the WHD investigator will generally not seek liquidated damages under the Act (described below) and the employer will certainly save resources that would otherwise be expended on potential litigation. The employer will also have the opportunity to obtain a legal release of claims and waiver of rights from the employees to whom any back pay amount is paid. If the parties are not able to resolve the finding of a violation, a determination will be made about whether litigation should ensue either through the DOL or by granting the individual employee his or her private right to sue.

Civil Litigation Under the Act

Actions by the DOL

When an employer is found to be in violation of the Act and the matter is not resolved, the WHD will pass the matter on to the DOL's litigation department, known as the Office of the Solicitor, to be considered for litigation in court. The Office of the Solicitor has about 500 lawyers who advise local offices regarding legal interpretations and handle litigation under the Act. The Solicitor of Labor is the chief legal officer of the DOL. In determining whether to file suit against an employer, the Office of the Solicitor will generally consider many factors, including the nature and severity of the violation, the employer's history of violations and the employer's conduct during the course of the investigation. More specifically, if the violation is particularly serious, involves a large number of employees or minors, or if it is not the employer's first offense, it is more likely that litigation will ensue. The solicitor will also consider whether the employer was believed to have concealed facts or falsified records during the course of the WHD investigation, which also makes litigation by the DOL much more likely.

Actions by the Aggrieved Employees

In the event that the DOL does not pursue civil litigation on behalf of an aggrieved employee, the employee will be given the right to sue on his or her own behalf in state or federal court. In addition, a group of similarly situated employees may sue an employer together. Although the vehicle of a standard "class action" under the Federal Rules of Civil Procedure is not available under the Fair Labor Standards Act, a similar mechanism known as a "collective action" is available. Similarly situated employees, which would include all those employees who have been adversely affected by an employer's violation of the Act, may bring a collective action to recover damages. Each such employee must give his or her specific consent, in writing, to such an action, which is then filed with the court. In recent years, the number of collective actions under the Act has exploded. The potential of large damage awards and attorneys fees is generally what drives such actions.

Corporate and Personal Liability for Violations

It is not uncommon for the DOL to name individuals as defendants in cases under the Act. This is because the Act broadly defines "employer" to include not just corporate entities, or what one would normally consider an "employer," but also any "person" who acts in the interest of the employer. As a practical matter, this means that even supervisors can be subject to personal liability for a violation of the Act. Because the Act allows for individual liability for violations, an individual defendant and the employer for whom they work can be held jointly and severally liable for any violations. Similarly, individuals who actively participate in an illegal act can be held personally liable for criminal violations of the Act.

Enforceability of Arbitration Agreements

It has become more and more commonplace for employers to require employees to sign agreements consenting to the "alternative dispute resolution" as the only means to resolve employment disputes. The federal courts have been flooded with litigation over the past several years concerning whether such agreements are enforceable. Generally, such agreements provide a terminal step of arbitration to resolve any employment claim of any kind, rather than allowing the employee to litigate the matter in a court. So long as the employee is not waiving any substantive right under the Act by consenting to an alternative dispute resolution process, the courts will normally enforce such agreements and require the employee to pursue arbitration. Accordingly, employers should consider whether the forum in which the complaints are heard is an important element of their relationship with their employees.

Statute of Limitations

Under most circumstances (in which there is no evidence of willful violation), the statute of limitations for bringing an action alleging a violation of the Act is two years. Willful violations of the Act carry a statute of limitations of three years. Making the distinction between a "willful" violation of the Act and a non-willful violation is obviously not a science and is extremely fact sensitive. According to the United States Supreme Court, the basic standard for making the determination is whether the employer either knew its conduct was prohibited by the Act or showed reckless disregard for the matter of whether its conduct was prohibited by the Act.

Defenses

The most commonly raised defense to an action under the Act is that the employer acted in "good faith." The good faith defense really comes in two different varieties:

- an employer may avoid payment of liquidated damages (discussed below) if it can prove that its acts or omissions were done in good faith and that it had a reasonable basis to believe that its actions were not in violation of the Act; and

- an employer may avoid back pay liability under the Act for minimum wage or overtime violations if it can show that its conduct was based on a good faith reliance on a ruling or rulings of the WHD or DOL regulations.

It is important to note that it is not sufficient to prove ignorance of the requirements of the Act in attempting to assert good faith. While the specific "white collar" exemptions to the overtime and minimum wage requirements of the Act are discussed elsewhere, for purposes of this chapter it should be noted that an employer will have the burden of proving the existence of facts to support an exemption as an affirmative defense.

Damages and Civil Penalties

Back Pay

As noted previously, in the event an employer is found to have violated the Act, it is liable to any aggrieved employee for the amount of unpaid wages. These types of damages may be sought by an individual employee, a group of employees in a "collective action" or by the DOL. In any case, the employer is responsible for the payment of these damages for whatever period of violation that can be proven within the statute of limitations.

Liquidated and Punitive Damages

In a suit to recover unpaid wages, the Act also authorizes the recovery of liquidated damages. Liquidated damages are considered to be an amount equal to the amount of back pay liability that an employee recovers. In other words, liquidated damages are essentially double damages. Employers are provided the opportunity to prove the "good faith" affirmative defense against the assessment of liquidated damages, as noted above. If an employer fails to prove the good faith defense, the award of liquidated damages in a wage lawsuit is automatic.

There are some courts that have recently held that in addition to liquidated damages under the Act, a successful plaintiff can also recover punitive damages in a retaliatory discharge case. Punitive damages are those damages which are authorized by the court to "punish" the employer for violating the law and to act as a deterrent to other potential violators of the Act.

Prejudgment and Post-Judgment Interest

Generally speaking, if a court has awarded liquidated damages to a plaintiff, prejudgment interest should not be awarded in the same case. The reasoning is that an award of prejudgment interest in addition to liquidated damages would be double compensation to the plaintiff for the same injury. However, prejudgment interest is not always available, even in cases in which liquidated damages are not awarded. If the lawsuit is initiated by the

DOL, some courts mandate that interest be granted, but others leave the matter to the discretion of the trial court. As with other civil judgments, post-judgment interest on an award under the Act is always available to the prevailing plaintiff.

Injunctive Relief

The DOL is empowered to bring an injunctive proceeding against an employer for purposes of enforcing the Act. Private litigants, who are suing on their own behalf, are not authorized by the Act to seek injunctive relief. The standard for issuing an injunction by a court is relatively stringent and so the use of the injunction is generally reserved for the most egregious cases. Moreover, the purposes of the injunction are to ensure that any violations are discontinued immediately and to put pressure on the employer to deter future violations.

Civil Penalties

In addition to the other damages obtainable under the Act, civil money penalties are available for repeated and willful violations of the Act. Civil penalties for violating the minimum wage and overtime provisions of the Act currently call for penalties of not more than $1,000 for each violation. (Violations of the child labor provisions may subject an employer to civil penalties of not more than $10,000 for each minor employee affected by the violation.) Generally, the assessment of the penalty will depend on whether the violation was repeated or willful or both. As its name suggests, a repeated violation occurs when an employer has previously been found by the WHD or a court to have violated the Act. A willful violation occurs when an employer knew that its conduct would violate the Act or if the employer showed reckless disregard for whether its conduct would violate the Act. The size of the penalty will be determined by the size of the employer, the severity of the violation found, the number of employees involved, whether the employer showed good faith, the employer's explanations and whether the employer commits to future compliance with the Act.

Once an employer is put on notice that a civil money penalty will be sought, it has a very short time period, 15 days after the receipt of the notice, to take "exception" to the determination. Failure to do so will result in a finding that the employer waived its right to have the penalty reviewed. Contesting the notice of civil penalty requires prompt action on the part of an employer, because the deadline is so short. Like other items of damages available to employees, the amount of the civil penalty can be negotiated with the Office of the Solicitor, but the employer should take special care to appeal the violation itself, not simply the amount of the penalty assessed.

Reasonable Attorneys' Fees

The Act allows, indeed mandates, the recovery of reasonable attorneys' fees in any private suit initiated by an employee. In the event that a judgment is obtained by an employee in a lawsuit to recover back wages, the court must also award attorneys' fees. It has been established for decades that the requirement of an award of reasonable attorneys' fees is mandatory on the court. The only matter that carries any level of discretion is the amount of attorneys' fees that will be awarded based on a "reasonableness" test. Different courts evaluate reasonableness in different ways, but it is well-settled that it is within the discretion of the trial court to ensure that the amount is "reasonable," given the issues in question and the amounts at stake.

Costs of the Action

The Act allows an employee to recover the costs of the action in addition to all of the other damages and attorneys' fees that are authorized. This item of recovery generally includes a wide array of things, such as document filing fees, trial witness fees, costs for copying documents, deposition costs, telephone expenses and the like. However, most courts have held that costs of the action do not include the recovery of expert witness fees and expenses.

Burdens of Proof and Persuasion

As in all civil cases, the burden of proof is on the plaintiff in cases arising under the Act. Whether it is the DOL or the employee, it is incumbent upon the plaintiff to establish a violation of the Act by a preponderance of the evidence. Many employers will be familiar with the "burden shifting" mechanisms of employment litigation under federal statutes such as Title VII of the Civil Rights Act of 1964. The Act does not provide for similar burden shifting.

On the other hand, in any case in which the employer asserts any affirmative defenses, such as good faith, it is incumbent upon the employer to establish that the affirmative defenses apply and have been proven, also by a preponderance of the evidence.

In criminal actions (discussed immediately below), the burden of proof is on the prosecution to prove beyond a reasonable doubt that the conduct violated the Act and that it was willful.

Criminal Actions

In addition to all the other issues that might face an employer who is found in violation of the Act, there is also the potential of criminal liability. A criminal action against an employer may be brought in conjunction with, or in lieu of, a civil action. The Act specifically provides that anyone who willfully violates the Act is subject to a criminal fine of no more than $10,000 and/or imprisonment for no more than six months. However, the Act has been expanded to provide that convictions may result in fines of more than $10,000 in certain situations. Unlike other enforcement actions, criminal actions under the Act are brought by the Attorney General of the United States, not the DOL. Also unlike civil cases, a criminal matter can be brought within five years, rather than the three-year statute of limitations for willful civil violations. A good faith defense is available in criminal proceedings just as it is in civil proceedings. It should be noted that actual criminal enforcement of the Act is relatively infrequent, although during investigations it is often made clear by the WHD investigator that such actions are possible.

Anti-Discrimination and Anti-Retaliation Provisions of the FLSA

In addition to all of the other protections of the Act, employers are also prohibited from terminating, or in any other way discriminating against, employees who have engaged in "protected activity" under the Act. It is of interest to note that every employer is covered by the requirements of the anti-discrimination provisions of the Act, whether they are covered by any other provision of the Act or not. If an employee can show that an adverse employment action was taken against him or her because of that employee's involvement in protected activity, the employer can be held liable. Generally, protected activities include things such as raising a complaint directly with the employer claiming that the Act was violated, filing a formal complaint against the employer with the DOL, instituting a court proceeding of any kind under the Act, or testifying on their behalf or on behalf of another plaintiff with respect to alleged violations of the Act. Even former employees can be protected under the Act. The most common alleged violation is a former employer giving an unfavorable reference to another potential employer (or attempting to "blacklist" a former employee) because they engaged in protected activity.

If an employer is found to have discriminated against or retaliated against an employee for engaging in protected activity, the remedies available generally include back pay, prejudgment interest (which is not available under other provisions of the Act), reinstatement to his or her former position or front pay, reasonable attorneys' fees, costs and such other legal or equitable relief as the court may determine appropriate and necessary.

Chapter 10
Wage-Hour Obligations of Government Contractors

Federal Laws and Regulations

Three major federal statues impose wage-hour obligations on companies doing business with the federal government. The Walsh-Healy Public Contracts Act applies to contracts to provide *materials and supplies* to the federal government. The McNamara-O'Hara Service Contract Act applies to contracts to provide *services* to the federal government. The Davis-Bacon Act applies to contracts for *construction*. All three statutes are administered by the United States Department of Labor and they apply to contracts with the United States federal government and the District of Columbia.

Each of these laws is summarized briefly below. Additional information can be found on the website of the United States Department of Labor (www.dol.gov), and in the Code of Federal Regulations (Walsh-Healy regulations at 41 CFR §§50-201, 202 and 206; McNamara-O'Hara regulations at 29 CFR Parts 4, 6 and 8; and Davis-Bacon regulations at 29 CFR Parts 1, 3 and 5)

Other federal laws extend the coverage of one or more of these statues to projects that are performed outside of the United States in localities such as U.S. territories. Any company contemplating performance of government contracts in U.S. territories should check in advance to determine whether any of these "wage-hour" statutes apply to the contract under consideration.

Walsh-Healy Public Contracts Act – Materials and Supplies

The Walsh-Healy Public Contracts Act (PCA) applies to contracts entered into by any agency or instrumentality of the United States government that exceeds or may exceed $10,000 in value for the manufacture or furnishing of materials, supplies, articles or equipment. Contracts not covered by the PCA include contracts for: purchases of materials, supplies, articles or equipment that may usually be bought in the "open market;" purchases of perishables; purchases of agricultural products from the original producers; contracts made by the Secretary of Agriculture for the purchase of agricultural commodities or products; contracts for public utility services and certain transportation and communication services; and supplies manufactured outside the U.S. (including Puerto Rico) or the Virgin Islands

Minimum Wage and Overtime Requirements

For many PCA contractors, the statute duplicates requirements to which they are already subject – the minimum wage and overtime requirements of the Fair Labor Standards Act (FLSA). For PCA contractors that are not already subject to the FLSA, they will need to begin to comply with the requirements that the federal minimum wage be paid to FLSA-"non-exempt" employees manufacturing or furnishing materials or supplies under the contract, and that a minimum of one and one-half (1½) times such a non-exempt employee's base rate of pay be paid to the employee for all hours worked by that employee in excess of 40 in a week. Compliance with the minimum wage and overtime provisions is enforced by the Wage-Hour Division (WHD) of the Employment Standards Administration of the Department of Labor (DOL).

Safety Provisions

The PCA also requires that work not be performed under unsanitary or hazardous conditions that are dangerous to the health and safety of employees. The health and safety provisions of the PCA are administered by the Occupational Safety and Health Administration (OSHA).

Employment of Certain Individuals Prohibited

The PCA generally prohibits the employment of convict labor and also prohibits employment of children less than 16 years of age. The PCA also prohibits employment of homeworkers (individuals who work at home producing goods for an employer), except in certain cases for handicapped clients of bona fide sheltered workshops.

Prime Contractors Liable for Sub-Contractors

Prime contractors (those who have contracts directly with the federal government that are covered by PCA) are responsible, and liable, for violations of the PCA committed by their secondary contractors (sub-contractors) who perform portions of the government contracts.

Notice to Employees

During the term of a contract covered by the PCA, an employer must post a notice that informs the employees of the basic requirements of the PCA. A copy of the notice (which also serves as a notice to satisfy several of the requirements of the McNamara-O'Hara Service Contract Act discussed below) may be obtained from the nearest DOL office, from OSHA or directly from the DOL website. The web address for the poster is: www.dol.gov/esa/regs/compliance/posters/pdf/govc.pdf

McNamara-O'Hara Service Contract Act – Services

The McNamara-O'Hara Service Contract Act (SCA) applies to every contract entered into by the United States or the District of Columbia when the principal purpose of the contract is to furnish services *in the United States* through the use of service employees. For purposes of the SCA, the United States includes any state, the District of Columbia and several territories and bases under the jurisdiction of the United States. The SCA does not apply to work performed on ships operating in international or foreign waters. If a portion of the contract is performed within the United

States and a portion is performed outside the United States, the SCA applies only to the portion performed in the United States.

The types of obligations a government contractor has under the SCA vary depending on the dollar value of the contract.

Contracts for $2,500 or Less

For service contracts that do not exceed $2,500 in value, the SCA requires only that employees working on such contracts be paid not less than the minimum wage specified in the FLSA. Of course, if the employer and the employees are otherwise covered by the FLSA, an SCA contractor with a contract worth less than $2,500 would also be required to comply with the overtime requirements of the FLSA.

Contracts in Excess of $2,500

The SCA requires that employees working on any service contract that exceeds $2,500 in value be paid the rates specified in the contract. The rates to be paid will be one of the following:

- the federal minimum wage, in the event that no specific wage determination has been made applicable to the contract;

- the wages and fringe benefits that the DOL has determined to be "prevailing" for the geographic area and the classification of work in which the employee is working (such wage determinations are to be available for public inspection during business hours at the Wage and Hour Division, Employment Standards Administration, U.S. Department of Labor. Copies are also made available on request at regional offices of the Wage and Hour Division);

- the wages and fringe benefits specified in a collective bargaining agreement of a predecessor employer who performed the contract immediately prior to the current contractor. In other words, if a government contractor bids upon and is awarded a contract under the SCA, the value of that contract exceeds $2,500 and the previous contractor performing that contract employed individuals who worked under a collective bargaining agreement that specified higher wages and fringe benefits than the prevailing wages set forth in the otherwise applicable wage determination, the higher wages and fringe benefits of the predecessor's collective bargaining agreement will apply. If the wages and fringe benefits set forth in such a collective bargaining agreement are "substantially at variance" with those in the prevailing wage determination, the contractor can request a hearing before the DOL to determine whether, instead, the prevailing wages in the wage determination shall apply;

◆ if a contractor employs someone in a classification for which no wage and/or fringe rate has been established, the SCA contractor is required to determine a wage and fringe rate for that classification, "slotting" it on to the wage and fringe scale where the contractor believes the classification fits based on a comparison of job duties. The rate, and the methodology by which the contractor determined it, are to be submitted to the contracting agency no later than 30 days after such an employee first performs work under the contract. The rate will then be approved, modified or disapproved by the DOL. The rate so determined by DOL must then be paid, effective with the first date any employee performed such work on the contract, requiring retroactive adjustments in the event the final rate is higher than the rate first established by the contractor.

Contracts in Excess of $100,000

Contracts under the SCA that exceed $100,000 in value are also subject to the Contract Work Hours and Safety Standards Act that requires payment of 1½ times the basic rate of pay for all hours worked on the contract in excess of 40 in a week. Again, if the employer involved is already subject to the FLSA, the overtime requirements are rules to which the contractor is already subject.

Safety and Health

The SCA contains similar safety and health provisions to those of the PCA described above. Specifically, if the contract is in excess of $2,500 in value, it may not be performed under unsanitary or hazardous conditions that are dangerous to the health or safety of service employees. Again, these provisions are administered by OSHA.

Notice to Employees

As in the case of the PCA, notice of the provisions of the SCA, and of the compensation required to be paid to employees under that contract, must be provided to employees in every workplace where the employees are working on a contract subject to the SCA, the dollar value of which exceeds $2,500. All notice provisions, other than the specific wage and fringe rates, are included on the poster referred to above in connection with the PCA.

Davis-Bacon Act – Construction

The Davis-Bacon Act (Davis-Bacon) applies to contracts with a value in excess of $2,000 with the United States and the District of Columbia for the construction, alteration or repair of public buildings or public works. In addition to Davis-Bacon, Congress has enacted a number of so-called "related Acts" involving construction in specific areas such as transportation, housing, air and water pollution reduction and health. If a particular construction project receives federal funds or assistance under more than one federal statute, the Davis-Bacon prevailing wage provisions will apply if *any* of the statutes involved requires observation of Davis-Bacon wage rates. Sub-contractors under any contract subject to Davis-Bacon are also covered by Davis-Bacon and a clause to that effect must be included in every sub-contract.

Davis-Bacon itself is limited geographically to the 50 states and the District of Columbia. However, some of the "related Acts" may provide for application of Davis-Bacon prevailing wage provisions in other areas, such as Guam or the Virgin Islands.

Davis-Bacon requires the payment of prevailing wages and fringe benefits to individuals employed "directly upon the site of the work" on construction projects to which Davis-Bacon applies. Davis-Bacon is administered by WHD. The wage determinations will set forth an amount of wages and an hourly value of fringe benefits. To meet the prevailing wages on a project, contractors need not pay wages and fringe benefits in the same proportion as set forth in the wage determinations so long as they pay a total hourly amount that equates to the total hourly wage and fringe benefits costs set forth in the wage determination.

Prevailing Wage Determinations

There are two basic types of prevailing wage determinations under Davis-Bacon. One is the "general" or "area" determination that establishes prevailing wage rates and fringe benefit rates for classifications of construction workers in an area in which a substantial amount of publicly funded construction activity is to take place. Such area wage determinations, once established, remain in effect until they are superceded by new area wage determinations, or until they are amended specifically by DOL. The other type of wage determination is a project wage determination. Project wage determinations are made whenever a contracting agency requests one that no area wage determination is applicable.

Types of Construction

In addition to the two types (area versus project) of wage determinations, separate wage determinations are made for different types of construction. Among the types of construction for which separate prevailing wage and fringe benefit determinations are made are: building construction (including buildings as well as some incidental grading and paving); residential construction (such as single family houses or apartment buildings of not more than four stories in height, including incidentals such as site work, parking areas, utilities, streets and sidewalks); heavy construction (such as water and sewer projects, dams, major bridges, flood control projects, waste water treatment facilities); highway construction (such as roads, streets, highways or other similar projects not incidental to residential, building or heavy construction). Demolition is not considered construction under the Davis-Bacon Act, but may be covered by the SCA. Landscaping is considered construction, but the rates for landscaping are likely to be derived from the nature of the projects with which it is connected, *i.e.,* building, residential, heavy or highway.

Wage Rates for Specific Crafts/Classifications

All area wage determinations will include all crafts/classifications for which sufficient data by type of construction are available in a given area. Project wage determinations will establish rates for all crafts/classifications the contracting agency believes are needed for the project for which the determination is being made.

Contractors interested in bidding on projects for which project wage determinations are being established should take care that all classifications necessary for the project are included in the determination. If not included in the original determination, such rates may be determined after the award of the bid and the beginning of work on the project, in which case the contractor may be obligated to different, higher rates than it anticipated when bidding and being awarded the project.

Determining the Rates

If a single rate of wages and fringe benefits is paid to more than 50 percent of the individuals working in a classification in an area, that will be the rate for that classification in that area. If such a single rate exists, it is often a rate specified in a collective bargaining agreement, thus leading frequently to the prevailing wage scale being the scale of wages set forth in construction collective bargaining agreements in a given area.

If no single rate is paid to more than 50 percent of the workers in a given classification in a given area, the DOL collects data concerning the various rates of wages and fringe benefits paid to such classification of worker and then uses the "weighted average" to determine the prevailing wage for the area and/or the project, whichever is applicable.

Bid documents for projects subject to Davis-Bacon should include either a copy of the applicable wage determination or information identifying the applicable wage determination so that the potential bidders can review it prior to submitting their bids. Additionally, area wage determinations are always available from the DOL. To access a database of current wage determinations, contractors can use the following Internet access procedure: go to *www.gpoaccess.gov*, and then click on the link identified as "A-Z Resource List," then click on the link to "Davis-Bacon Wage Determinations."

Schedule for New Wage Determinations

From the DOL website, contractors and potential contractors can also obtain information concerning the schedule the DOL intends to follow in making new area wage determinations. By utilizing this process, interested parties have an opportunity to submit information to the DOL to be considered. Such information is important for both the "single rate paid to more than 50 percent" of the workers, and the "weighted average" method of establishing a prevailing wage rate.

Weekly Pay and Payroll Certification Required

Davis-Bacon contractors are required to pay employees the prevailing wages and benefits on a weekly basis, and are required by the Copeland Anti-Kickback Act and its regulations to complete a form, executed by an authorized officer or employee of the contractor who supervises payment of wages, verifying the payment of the prevailing wages called for by the contract and Davis-Bacon. These statements are to be delivered weekly to a designated representative of the contracting agency.

Site of the Work

The Davis-Bacon Act provides specifically that the individuals who are entitled to the prevailing wages are those "employed directly upon the site of the work." Disputes over the meaning of "site of the work" spawned significant litigation over the past decade. The current rules defining the site of the work are found in Department of Labor Regulations located at 29 C.F.R. Part 5, Subpart A, § 5.2 (l).

Notice to Employees

Every employer performing work covered by Davis-Bacon (and related acts) must post a notice that includes any applicable wage determination at the site of the work. The notice must be posted in a prominent, accessible place. The poster may be downloaded from the following website: www.dol.gov/esa/rags/compliance/posters/pdf/fedprojc.pdf

Indiana "Common Construction Wage" Law

An Indiana statute generally referred to as the Common Construction Wage Law can be found at Ind. Code 5-16-7-1, *et seq.* It requires that any contractor awarded a contract valued at $150,000 or more by the state of Indiana or any political subdivision or municipal corporation of the state of Indiana, for construction of a public work must pay "for each class of work...a scale of wages that may not be less than the common construction wage." A "public work" includes a "public building, highway, street, ally, bridge, sewer, drain, improvement or any other work of any nature or character whatsoever, which is paid for out of public funds" except, contracts let by the Indiana Department of Transportation for the construction of highways, streets and bridges. (Ind. Code 8-23-9 applies to such projects).

The current version of the Indiana Common Construction Wage Law was enacted in 1995. It is a successor to what was known as the "prevailing wage law" enacted originally in 1935. Challenges to various aspects of the

1995 version of the statute resulted in decisions of the Indiana Court of Appeals, clarifying certain elements of the statute. One clarification is that reference to a common construction "wage" in the statute is to be interpreted as applying to both "wages and benefits." Another point of clarification made in a recent decision of an Indiana Court of Appeals is that "common" means "mode" (most frequently occurring) not "average" or "mean."

Procedure for Determining Common Construction Wage

The common construction wage is to be determined for each project subject to the statute. The Indiana Department of Labor is to schedule a wage determination meeting at the request of the agency planning to award the project. The common construction wage scale for a project is to be determined by a committee established for the project. The common wage committee is to consist of five individuals as follows: a labor representative (appointed by the president of the state Federation of Labor); an industry representative (appointed by the awarding agency); a member to be named by the governor (usually from the Indiana Department of Labor); two taxpayers who pay taxes that will be the funding source for the project and who live in the county of the project (one appointed by the awarding agency and one appointed by the county legislative body).

The committee is required by statute to meet and determine the classifications of labor to be employed on the project, divided into three groups: skilled labor, semi-skilled labor and unskilled labor. This is a two-step process. The first step is to classify the labor to be employed by determining the trades or crafts to be utilized on the project. The second step is to set wages for skilled, semi-skilled and unskilled workers within each trade or craft so determined.

The second step is accomplished by convening a meeting subject to the Indiana Open Door Law and inviting presentation of information to determine the wage rates common to the area in which the project is located. The statute states "the committee is not required to consider information not presented to the committee at the meeting," but apparently does not prohibit consideration of information not presented to the committee at the meeting. The committee must then establish the scale of wages for the projects at "not...less than the common construction wage...currently being paid in the county where the project is located."

Further information concerning Indiana's Common Construction Wage Law can be found in the Indiana Code (Ind. Code 5-16-7-1 *et seq.*), the Indiana Administrative Code (50IAC11-4-1 *et seq.*) and on the Indiana Department of Labor website (www.in.gov/labor). Additionally, the Indiana Department of Labor has included for download from its website a Common Construction Wage Implementation Manual entitled "Guide to Establishing the Common Construction Wage."

Chapter 11
Equal Pay Act

Background of Statute

The Equal Pay Act (EPA) was enacted in 1963 as an amendment to the FLSA, one year before Congress passed Title VII of the Civil Rights Act of 1964, which prohibits employment discrimination on the basis of race, sex, religion, national origin or color. Unlike Title VII, the EPA is aimed only at sex discrimination. In simple terms, the EPA requires that male and female employees receive "equal pay for equal work." The concept of "equal" work does not mean identical work, but only substantially equal work. The EPA is only applicable in the context of male and female employees employed in the same job. It is not a "comparable worth" law that attempts to measure the value of one job against another.

Unlike the basic minimum wage and overtime provisions of the FLSA, which are administered by the Department of Labor, the EPA is administered and enforced by the Equal Employment Opportunity Commission (EEOC), and the EEOC has promulgated regulations under the EPA.

Requirements of Equal Pay Act

The Equal Pay Act prohibits an employer from paying employees in the same job in the same establishment differently based on sex. The law states:

> No employer having employees subject to any provisions of this section shall discriminate, within any establishment in which such employees are employed, between employees on the basis of sex by paying wages to employees in such establishment at a rate less than the rate at which he pays wages to employees of the opposite sex in such establishment for equal work on jobs the performance

of which requires equal skill, effort, and responsibility, and which are performed under similar working conditions, except where such payment is made pursuant to (i) a seniority system; (ii) a merit system; (iii) a system which measures earnings by quantity or quality of production; or (iv) a differential based on any other factor other than sex . . . .

The EPA also prohibits an employer who is paying different rates in violation of the statute from reducing the wage rate of any employee in order to bring itself into compliance. Thus, if an employer discovers it may be in violation of the EPA, to remedy the situation it must increase the pay of the lower-paid employee(s).

> **Example:** An employer discovers that it has a male employee performing a job at $10.00 per hour and a female employee performing the same job at $9.50 per hour. Assuming there is no EAP-approved justification for the difference, the employer must raise the pay rate of the female employee to $10.00 per hour, rather than reduce the rate of the male employee.

An employer is prohibited from discharging or disciplining an employee because the employee made an EPA complaint to EEOC, filed suit alleging a violation of the EPA or testified in an EPA proceeding.

Employers Covered

The Equal Pay Act applies to all employees engaged in commerce or the production of goods for commerce and all employees of enterprises that are engaged in interstate commerce or the production of goods for interstate commerce, all as defined in the FLSA. It also applies to labor organizations and state and local governments.

Elements of Equal Pay Act Violation

There are four requisite elements of an EPA violation. It must be proven that the employer pays male and female employees (i) who perform equal work (ii) in the same establishment (iii) different wage rates (iv) on the basis of sex. The complaining employee has the burden of proving each of these elements.

Same Establishment

The focus of the EPA is on each "establishment" of the employer. Generally, each separate place of business is considered to be a separate establishment. Thus, employers with places of business in different locations do not have to pay the same wage rates at all of their places of business.

There are, however, circumstances in which more than one place of business might collectively be regarded as one "establishment," such as if there is centralized control and management (*e.g.,* hiring, setting of wage rates, etc.), interchange of employees between the places of business and other such factors. Conversely, in other circumstances two or more parts of a business may be regarded as different establishments even if they are physically located in the same place (such as functionally separate operations that are separately managed).

Unequal Pay

An EPA plaintiff must establish that he or she is paid less wages or at a lesser wage rate than an employee of the opposite sex. In determining the "wages" paid, all remuneration for work performed is considered (including wages, commission, bonus, profit sharing, fringe benefits, etc.).

That a difference in pay is established by a collective bargaining agreement is no defense to an EPA violation.

Difference in Pay Based on Sex

An individual's initial burden of establishing the "basis of sex" element of an EPA violation is met by showing that one employee of the opposite sex is paid more than the complaining employee, even if there are other employees of the opposite sex who are paid less than the complaining employee. The burden is then on the employer to establish that the difference is based on some factor other than sex.

Example: An employer has four welders on its staff – one male welder paid $11.00 per hour, one female welder paid $10.00 per hour and two male welders paid $9.00 per hour. The female welder can establish the "basis of sex" element of an EPA violation by showing that a male welder is paid $1.00 per hour more than she, even though two male welders are paid $1.00 per hour less than she.

Work Must be Equal

The names given to jobs are not controlling as to whether work is equal. There are four factors involved in determining whether the work performed by two individuals is equal for EPA purposes. A difference in any one of the four factors establishes that the work is not equal, even if all three of the other factors are equal.

Similar Working Conditions

Comparison jobs for EPA purposes must be performed under similar working conditions. In determining whether working conditions are similar, the focus is on factors such as the place the work is performed (*e.g.*, outside or inside); differences in exposure to elements, hazards and unpleasant working environment; and differences in time (although this does not include a difference in shifts). That two employees may work in different departments does not necessarily mean that their working conditions are not similar for EPA purposes. Slight or inconsequential differences in working conditions do not justify a difference in pay.

> **Example:** An EPA analysis would ordinarily not compare an inside salesperson to an outside salesperson.

Equal Skill

The evaluation of whether jobs involve equal skill requires looking at factors such as the experience, training, education and ability required to perform the job. The focus is not on the qualifications of the persons actually performing the jobs. The respective qualifications of those persons are irrelevant in determining whether the work requires equal skills. The skills required by jobs may be found to be equal even if one employee may not have to exercise all of the skills to the extent or as frequently as the employee in another job.

Equal Effort

The EPA requirement that the jobs involve equal effort focuses on the physical or mental exertion required for performance of the jobs. The occasional performance of extra physical or mental effort does not necessarily lead to the conclusion that jobs do not require equal effort. Furthermore, jobs may be considered to require equal effort even if the kind of effort they require is different (*e.g.*, pace versus strength required).

Equal Responsibility

This component of the equal work analysis examines the degree of accountability required in performing the job. Although this is a somewhat more subjective factor than the other factors described above, the consideration includes such things as whether the employee works independently, supervises others (and, if so, how many), is entrusted with decision-making authority, is responsible for the financial affairs of the employer and the like. The breadth of responsibility of the positions is also a relevant consideration. For example, a manager position in charge of three departments may be considered to require greater responsibility than a manager position of only one department.

Exceptions to EPA Requirements

The Equal Pay Act provides four specific exceptions to the general requirement that employers pay male and female employees equal pay for equal work. The exceptions do not, however, come into play unless the positions being compared are first found to be equal in terms of effort, skill and responsibility, and to be performed under similar working conditions. Thus, the exceptions are defenses to what would otherwise be a violation of the EPA and, accordingly, the employer has the burden of proving that one or more of the exceptions is applicable.

The four exceptions are if a difference in pay is made pursuant to a seniority system, a merit system, a system which measures earnings by quantity or quality of production, or the catch-all "any other factor other than sex." In order to establish one of the "system" exceptions, it is not necessary that it be a formal or written system. What is required is that there is an established plan or system in place that has been communicated to the affected employees and applied equally to employees of both sexes.

Seniority System

An employer is free to compensate employees who perform equal work differently based upon their relative tenure with the employer. In order for length of service to justify a differential in payment, however, the system or plan must be applied the same to male and female employees.

Merit System

This EPA exception involves the employer's utilization of a system or process that evaluates employees according to pre-determined criteria and then bases their pay on their evaluations. The evaluation system must be one that is consistently utilized and administered uniformly. Evaluations based on subjective criteria are less likely to succeed as an EPA defense than those based on objective criteria.

> **Example:** It is not an EPA violation for an employer to pay a greater rate to a female employee, who received an "exceeds expectations" evaluation, than it pays to a male employee in the same job who received only a "meets expectations" evaluation.

System that Measures Earning by Quantity or Quality of Production

Another EPA exception is if a difference in payment is attributable to a system that measures earnings by quantity or quality of production. This exception generally refers to incentive or piecework systems that base an employee's compensation on objective and quantifiable standards (such as number of pieces produced per shift or per hour). As with other EPA-approved systems, such system must be uniformly applied to both male and female employees.

Differential Based on any Other Factor Other than Sex

Since the EPA is specially directed at sex discrimination, this exception is a catch-all that acknowledges that any difference in pay based on any factor other than sex is lawful. In some respects, the analysis of this exception may overlap with the analysis of the elements of an EPA violation. As an example, a difference based on one job being more strenuous than the other is a factor other than sex, but may also establish that the jobs do not require equal effort. The difference in the approach taken is a significant one. If viewed as an element of the EPA violation, the complaining employee bears the burden of proof. If viewed as an exception to the EPA requirements, the employer bears the burden of proving it.

Examples of factors that have been found to be an "other factor other than sex" so as to fall within this EPA exception include temporary assignments (in which a higher-paid employee retains his/her regular rate of pay while temporarily assigned to a lesser-paying job), "red circle" rates, shift differential, external market forces (*e.g.*, competition from other employers or an applicant's prior salary history); and superior education or work experience.

As with all EPA exceptions, a factor relied upon to establish a "factor other than sex" defense must be one that is uniformly applied and will not succeed if it is shown that the factor has only benefited employees of one sex.

Enforcement and Remedies Under the Equal Pay Act

Since the EPA was enacted as part of the Fair Labor Standards Act, the procedures for asserting EPA claims follow those of the FLSA. Suits for violation of the EPA can be brought by employees or by the Equal Employment Opportunity Commission on behalf of employees.

Private Parties

Employees are free to institute suits for EPA violations directly in court. Class actions are also allowable. Unlike most other non-discrimination statutes, EPA plaintiffs are not required to exhaust administrative remedies with EEOC or any other agency before bringing suit. Employees can bring an action for back pay and damages for violation of the EPA, as well as for retaliatory action taken against the employee for asserting his or her rights under the EPA. An employee's right to sue individually terminates if EEOC has filed suit on the employee's behalf or on behalf of other employees similarly situated to the employee.

Equal Employment Opportunity Commission

The EEOC is charged with the administration and enforcement of the EPA and has broad investigative powers. The EEOC may also sue an employer for wages and damages on behalf of one or more employees and may also seek injunctive relief to restrain future violations of the EPA.

Relief Available

An employer found to have violated the EPA is liable for back pay to the affected employee(s), plus "liquidated damages" in an equal amount if it is found that the employer's violation was willful. Generally, the standard for whether an employer's violation was willful is whether the employer knew or showed reckless disregard for whether its conduct violated the EPA. Prevailing EPA plaintiffs are also entitled to attorney's fees and court costs. Plaintiffs (individuals or the EEOC) in an EPA action are entitled to a trial by jury as to claims for back wages.

An employer found to have willfully and flagrantly violated the EPA may also be subject to criminal fines, imprisonment or both.

Employees who have been terminated or retaliated against by an employer in violation of the EPA may be entitled to reinstatement, as well as payment of lost wages, liquidated damages, attorney's fees and court costs. Some courts have also allowed the recovery of compensatory and punitive damages in EPA retaliation cases.

Statute of Limitations

An EPA action must be brought within two years of the violation or three years in the case of a willful violation.

Chapter 12

Wage Garnishment in Indiana

Introduction

In today's business world, employers are faced with a wide range of legal obligations to deduct funds from the earnings of their employees. An employer must withhold federal, state and local taxes. In addition, employers may be required to make other deductions for payment of delinquent taxes, support of children or former spouses, repayment of student loans or satisfaction of a number of debts to others.

This process – called garnishment, generally – is complex and can be hazardous to employers. Both state and federal statutes are involved and these statutes are not integrated and, even more importantly, usually do not provide clear answers to the basic sorts of questions with which employers are faced. Even courts and administrative agencies often do not understand the complexities of garnishment law. In this chapter, it is our intention to provide you a summary of existing law applicable to Indiana employers as of the publication date. This chapter will hardly serve to answer all possible garnishment questions, but it will provide a reliable guide to describe many garnishment-related transactions. For specific advice in situations that are not clearly addressed, employers should seek legal advice from qualified counsel.

A Glossary of Key Terms Relating to Wage Garnishment

Disposable Earnings - The terms "disposable earnings," "disposable income," and "disposable pay" are used in various statutes governing garnishment. All of these terms are defined as that part of the compensation of an individual from an employer remaining after the deduction of any amounts required by law. Thus, practically speaking, this is the amount left after the withholding of current federal income, Social Security, Medicare, state income and local income taxes. Any voluntary deductions – such as elective retirement plan contributions – are not used to determine disposable earnings.

For the purpose of determining disposable earnings, an employer should include salary, wages and commissions.

Exempt Pay - The term "exempt pay" applies to Internal Revenue Service (IRS) levies. Exempt pay is that amount which the employer must pay each pay period to the employee. The remaining wages (after required withholding for current federal, state and local taxes) is to be paid to the IRS in satisfaction of the tax levy. Exempt pay is determined by applying the rules published by the IRS in its Publication 1494.

Garnishment – "Garnishment" refers to a legal procedure in which a creditor is permitted to satisfy a delinquent debt by seizing the debtor's money or property that is in the possession of a third person. The term is also used in Indiana and other states to describe a procedure in which courts place a lien on a defendant's property in the hands of third parties. The purpose of this sort of court-ordered pre-judgment garnishment is to preserve the property that would be used to pay a plaintiff's judgment if the defendant loses the lawsuit. Pre-judgment garnishment <u>never</u> applies to wages. Within the term "garnishment" is the concept of wage garnishment, defined as a legal or equitable procedure by which the earnings of an individual are required to be withheld by a garnishee (the employer) for the payment of any debt.

Guaranty Agency - This term applies to student loan default garnishments. A "guaranty agency" is a state government agency or a private not-for-profit corporation that is empowered to administer a federal student loan program on behalf of the federal government. Guaranty agencies are empowered by federal law to directly garnish wages for repayment of a federally guaranteed student loan. Although each state has only one guaranty agency, a single guaranty agency may cover several states and <u>any</u> guaranty agency may garnish wages in any state. The current list of guaranty agencies with garnishment power is available at: http://www.ed.gov/offices/OPE/guaranty.html

Wage Garnishment

The central focus of this chapter is wage garnishment, which we have defined as a legal or equitable procedure by which a third-person garnishee (usually an employer) is required to withhold and remit amounts from the earnings of an individual. Although there are several different categories of wage garnishment, each governed by a different set of rules and, often, by separate procedures, all wage garnishments share a common framework:

- There must be notice to the employer.

- Based upon an order of some sort, a deduction from wages occurs.

- Remittance is made to an official entity such as a court or administrative agency.

- Provision is made for the continuation or termination of garnishment in subsequent pay periods.

There are a number of ways in which an employer may incur liability for an error in a wage garnishment. For example, by ignoring a valid garnishment order or honoring an invalid garnishment order, an employer may incur liability to the creditor or the debtor. Additionally, by garnishing too little or too much and even by failing to initiate garnishment quickly enough, an employer may incur liability. Unfortunately, employers are allowed very little margin for error in wage garnishment.

As a consequence of these risks and to avoid the pitfalls associated with wage garnishment, an employer must establish standard procedures to insure that each garnishment document received is quickly and accurately processed. To do this, each employer's comprehensive wage garnishment procedure should include the following steps:

- Identify garnishment documents immediately upon delivery.

- Verify the employment of the person named in the garnishment document.

- Determine the category of the wage garnishment document.

- Verify that the garnishment document was issued by a court or administrative agency with authority to garnish wages in Indiana.

- Inform the employee of the receipt of the garnishment document.

- Determine whether any other garnishment orders are currently effective against the employee.

- Establish the relative priority of multiple garnishment orders.

- Determine the amount to be garnished.

- Withhold the proper amount.

- Pay the amount withheld to the Clerk of the Court or to the garnishing agency.

- Maintain a receipt, cancelled check or other evidence of payment.

- Continue withholding until the order is satisfied or rescinded.

- Inform the court or agency if the employee's employment is terminated.

Dealing with Categories of Wage Garnishment

The Categories of Wage Garnishment

There are seven different categories of wage garnishment that an employer may encounter:

- bankruptcy wage deduction orders

- Internal Revenue Service tax levies

- child support orders

- spouse support orders

- judgment debt garnishments

- Indiana tax garnishments

- student loan default garnishments

In this chapter, each of these garnishment categories will be described in detail with particular attention to the following characteristics of each category:

- The courts or agencies legally entitled to issue each garnishment category.

- The form or format of a valid order for each garnishment category.

- The method for determining the proper amount to be withheld.

- Special problems and concerns for each garnishment category.

Bankruptcy Wage Deduction Orders

Bankruptcy Wage Deduction Orders are a part of an employee's Chapter 13 bankruptcy plan. A valid Bankruptcy Wage Deduction Order may be issued by a United States Bankruptcy Court anywhere in the United States and will be signed by a bankruptcy judge. Such an order will require the employer to deduct a specific sum from the employee's wages every pay period for a term of three to five years. The order will direct that the deducted funds be paid to a Chapter 13 trustee for eventual payment to the employee's creditors. The amount to be deducted may be as large as the bankruptcy court wishes. There is no legal deduction limit except that all withholding for current federal, state and local taxes must be satisfied before the Chapter 13 deduction is made. The employer should continue to honor the Chapter 13 order until a termination or modification order is received from the same court. If the employee's employment is terminated, the employer should immediately inform the Chapter 13 trustee listed in the order.

The balance of the employee's wages, after normal withholding and the Chapter 13 deduction, are paid directly to the employee. This balance is not generally subject to any other garnishment. Most Chapter 13 Wage Deduction Orders specifically prohibit any other categories of garnishment while the order is in effect. Some Chapter 13 orders prohibit all other garnishments except Child Support Garnishment Orders. It is important to read the terms of each Chapter 13 order to determine which other garnishments are permitted.

Internal Revenue Service Tax Levies

The IRS is authorized by federal law to garnish wages for payment of delinquent taxes. IRS garnishments usually do not involve a court order. Instead the IRS issues a Form 668-W "Notice of Levy on Wages, Salary and Other Income." An employer must begin deductions immediately upon receipt of the levy, including deduction from wages already earned but not yet paid to the employee. The amount to be deducted each pay period is determined by consulting IRS publication 1494. Publication 1494 is a one-page chart that shows the exempt amount of wages that must be paid to an employee based on filing status and number of claimed tax exemptions. The nonexempt balance of the employee's wages (less current federal, state and local taxes) must be paid to the IRS.

Child Support Deduction Orders and Spouse Support Deduction Orders

Child and Spouse Support Deduction Orders (support orders) are orders issued by courts or by state government agencies in the name of courts. Child Support Deduction Orders are usually issued on standard forms rather than as court orders. Spouse Support Deduction Orders have become very rare because the laws of most states no longer encourage alimony. Consequently, a Spouse Support Deduction Order will probably appear as a conventional court order rather than a standard form. Both types of support orders from any court or state support agency in the United States and its possessions are always immediately effective in Indiana. An employer must begin deductions immediately upon receipt of a support order, unless the order allows a delay explicitly.

The amount to be deducted is the lesser of the dollar amount specified in the support order, or the maximum support order deduction allowed by federal and Indiana law. The formulas used to determine the maximum allowable deduction are as follows:

- If the employee is supporting a current spouse or dependent child and is ordered to support an ex-spouse or different dependent child, 50 percent of weekly disposable earnings can be taken.

- If the employee is not currently supporting a spouse or child other than those referred to in the support order, then 60 percent of disposable earnings can be taken.

In either case (50 percent or 60 percent), an additional 5 percent of the disposable earnings can be taken for arrearages more than 12 weeks old.

As a general rule, employers should use the 60 percent deduction limit. It is up to the court to inform the employer if the employee is in arrears requiring an extra five percent deduction. It is up to the employee to convince the court that support of current dependents merits use of the 50 percent deduction.

When a support order directs an additional deduction for payment of arrearages, the employer must keep track of these extra deductions in order to determine when the arrearages are satisfied. Ideally, the issuing court or agency should recognize satisfaction of the arrearages by issuing a new order reducing the total deduction. In practice, no new order is usually issued unless the employer or the employee requests one. Employers should request written instructions from the court or state agency before the arrearages are fully paid.

The only effective difference between a Child Support Deduction Order and a Spouse Support Deduction Order is the priority each is accorded when multiple garnishments are issued affecting the same employee. The impact of these differing priorities is addressed in this chapter.

Judicial Debt Garnishment Orders

A Judicial Debt Garnishment Order is issued by an Indiana court or (in rare instances) by a federal court. Judicial Debt Garnishment Orders are used to force payment of any prior court judgment. Such orders commonly enforce the satisfaction of consumer debt, civil damages or unpaid rent. Employers should verify that the order issues from a court and is not merely an official looking document prepared by a creditor without garnishment authority. All funds deducted should be paid to the clerk of the issuing court, never to the creditor or any private person.

In Indiana, judicial garnishment proceedings are especially hazardous for employers. An employer cannot wait for a formal court order to begin deductions for a judicial garnishment. The deductions must begin as soon as the employer receives any notice that a garnishment action has been filed. Such notice will usually be a summons and a questionnaire bearing the title "Interrogatories." Indiana courts hold employers liable for all deductions that could have been made from the date notice arrives. Some courts have held employers liable for funds that could have been deducted from paychecks already prepared even when notice was received on the day prior to payday. This liability can be expensive when an employee quits or declares bankruptcy. In such cases, an employer may be required to pay to the employee's creditor, from the employer's own funds, the full amount it should have deducted.

The amount to be deducted for a judicial debt garnishment is determined by a formula established by both Indiana and federal law. For any workweek, the employer must withhold the lesser of.

- Twenty-five percent of the employee's disposable earnings; or

- the amount that the employee's disposable earnings exceed 30 times the federal minimum hourly wage. The federal minimum wage is currently $5.15 and, thus, this exempt amount is $154.50 per week.

For pay periods other than the week, subrule (b), above, is modified proportionally.

Indiana Tax Garnishments

Garnishment for delinquent Indiana state taxes differs significantly from the IRS levy procedure. When a taxpayer becomes delinquent in the payment of Indiana income taxes or other state taxes (such as sales tax), the Indiana Department of Revenue will issue a tax warrant that may be sent to the sheriff of the Indiana county in which the taxpayer resides. Upon receipt of a warrant, the sheriff is empowered to seize and sell the taxpayer's property to satisfy the tax obligation. The sheriff may also garnish the taxpayer's wages either by obtaining a court order under same procedure as for the judicial Debt Garnishment Order or by issuing a garnishment order upon his own authority.

If the sheriff is unsuccessful in collecting the amount due under a tax warrant, the matter may be returned to the Indiana Department of Revenue. The Indiana Code gives the Department of Revenue the power to garnish the taxpayer's wages with only an administrative notice. The department is not required to obtain a court order. At the present time, the Indiana Department of Revenue does not exercise this direct garnishment power. Instead, uncollected warrants are referred to private attorneys. An action initiated by one of these attorneys may result in the entry of a judicial Debt Garnishment Order addressed to the taxpayer's employer.

Whether an Indiana Tax Garnishment Order is issued by a sheriff, by a court or by the Department of Revenue, the amount of deduction is determined using the same rule as for judicial Debt Garnishment Orders.

Student Loan Default Garnishments

Garnishment orders for repayment of defaulted student loans present some problems of verification. Under federal law, no court order is required. Instead, these orders may be issued by the U.S. Department of Education or by any federally accredited state guaranty agency. (A garnishment order issued by the state student loan guaranty agency of any state is valid in Indiana, provided that it invokes the authority of federal law.) Some of these orders may present a very non-legal appearance, looking more like letters on a guaranty agency's letterhead. If an order is not issued directly from the

U.S. Department of Education, an employer should verify that the issuing agency is in fact an official guaranty agency, by consulting the list posted by the Department of Education on the Internet at: http://www.ed.gov/ offices/OPE/guaranty.html

This verification is essential because a substantial number of student loan garnishment orders have been issued by companies that are not actually guaranty agencies but are debt collection contractors. Orders issued by such contractors are not valid. Any garnishment based on such an invalid order could obligate the employer to reimburse the employee for the amount withheld, plus punitive damages and attorneys fees.

Student Loan Default Garnishments Orders will specify the amount to be deducted from the employee's wages as a percentage of disposable earnings. This specified amount is usually 10 percent of disposable earnings. (Federal law permits the U.S. Department of Education (but not state guaranty agencies) to garnish up to 15 percent of disposable earnings for repayment of student loans. There is no current indication that the Department of Education intends to use this higher garnishment limit.) However, the employer must ensure that the amount deducted is also less than the upper limit established for judicial Debt Garnishment Orders.

Invalid Wage Garnishment Orders

Garnishment orders (except Child Support Deduction Orders and Spouse Support Deduction Orders) of state courts outside Indiana do not have the force of law in this state. An Indiana employer must refuse to obey a judicial garnishment order issued by a non-Indiana state court. Such out-of-state orders must be "domesticated" in Indiana. When a creditor secures domestication, the result will be a judicial Debt Garnishment Order issued by an Indiana court. This domesticated order must, then, be obeyed. As a general rule, employers should refuse to respond to garnishment interrogatories received from courts in other states until they have consulted legal counsel.

Garnishment demands from businesses, private persons and collection agencies should never be honored unless they have been submitted to an Indiana court or a federal court and have resulted in the issuance of an order signed by a judge or magistrate that specifically directs garnishment.

Only a few government agencies have the authority to garnish wages without a court order. The only agencies apparently having such power are the following:

- The U.S. Internal Revenue Service

- The Indiana Department of Revenue

- Sheriffs of counties in Indiana (when enforcing Indiana tax warrants)

- The child support enforcement agencies of each of the states

- The U.S. Department of Education

- State student loan guaranty agencies

Bankruptcy trustees do not have the power to garnish wages without a court order.

Dealing with Multiple Garnishments

The Problem of Multiple Garnishments

An additional difficulty arises when an employer receives two or more orders to garnish the same employee's wages. This situation arises fairly frequently because an employee in financial difficulty is likely to have several creditors seeking payment of delinquent debt. In almost all multiple garnishment cases, there will be insufficient funds in each paycheck to satisfy every demand.

The Priority Among the Categories of Garnishment

There is an established priority among garnishment orders as follows:

Priority 1:   Chapter 13 Bankruptcy Wage Deduction Orders

Priority 2:   Child Support Deduction Orders (issued prior to an IRS levy)

Priority 3:   Internal Revenue Service Tax Levies

Priority 4:   Child Support Orders (issued after an IRS levy)

Priority 5:   Judicial Debt Garnishment Orders

Spouse Support Deduction Orders

Indiana Tax Garnishments

Student Loan Default Garnishments

(The four categories in Priority 5 are of equal priority. Among these four categories, specific priority is determined based on date of issue. The oldest garnishment order within these four categories enjoys the highest precedence.)

The Rules for Multiple Garnishments

There are several rules that an employer should observe in applying these priorities.

- **Rule 1:** A higher priority garnishment is always paid prior to a lower priority garnishment regardless of the date of issue or date of receipt. Even if a lower priority order has been honored for one or more pay periods before a higher priority order is received, the higher priority order enjoys precedence.

- **Rule 2:** Within the same priority level, the earliest dated order is always paid first.

• **Rule 3:** In each pay period the maximum allowable deduction will be made for the highest priority garnishment.

• **Rule 4:** For the next priority garnishment, perform the following steps:

  • Determine the garnishment limit for this garnishment based on the employee's total disposable income before all garnishments.

  • Compare the total amount already garnished in the present pay period for all higher priority garnishments to the limit for this garnishment.

  • If the total amount already garnished is greater than the limit for this garnishment, make no deduction.

  • If the total amount already garnished is less than the limit for this garnishment, deduct the amount that makes the overall total exactly equal the limit for this garnishment.

• **Rule 5:** Repeat the application of Rule 4 for each additional garnishment order in the exact order of priority.

  Note: There is one exception to Rules 4 and 5. When two or more Child Support Deduction Orders are filed against the same employee, all of these Child Support Deduction Orders share in the amount garnished on a pro rata basis. This pro rata exception applies only to Child Support Deduction Orders.

• **Rule 6:** Any court or agency whose garnishment order is not fully satisfied due to these priorities should be informed of the reason. This will usually avoid legal action against the employer.

Examples of Multiple Garnishments

Example 1: Employee A earns $500 per week from which an initial deduction is made in the amount of $125 for federal, state and local taxes, leaving disposable earnings of $375. A has no voluntary deductions from wages. In week 1, the employer B receives a summons in an action for judicial debt garnishment to collect a debt of $1,000. Although B has not received a garnishment order, B must begin withholding as soon as he receives notice. At this time there are no other garnishments affecting A. B must deduct $93.75, which is the lesser of

- 25% of disposable earnings (0.25 X $375 = $93.75), and

- the amount of disposable earnings in excess of $154.50 per week ($375 - $154.50 = $220.50)

Example 2: The facts are as described in Example 1. In Week 2, B receives a Child Support Deduction Order garnishing A's wages. The Child Support Deduction Order requires B to garnish $250 per week. B determines correctly that the Child Support Deduction Order holds a higher priority than the judicial debt garnishment received in Week 1, so the Child Support Deduction Order must be paid first. The amount to be deducted for the Child Support Deduction Order is $225, which is less than the order demands. However, as a general rule, the child support deduction is limited to 60% of disposable earnings. (0.60 X $375= $225)

The judicial debt garnishment remains in effect but the employer may not make a deduction for it in week 2. A deduction for this lower priority garnishment can be made only if the sum of the two deductions is less than the limit for the second garnishment. However, the amount deducted for child support already exceeds the limit for judicial debt garnishment.

Example 3: The facts are as described in Examples 1 and 2, except A is able to have his Child Support Deduction Order modified. The old Child Support Deduction Order is rescinded and a new one is issued, requiring a deduction of only $40 per week. The new Child Support Deduction Order is still higher priority than the judicial debt garnishment, but B must now deduct for both garnishments. The child support deduction must be made in the full amount of $40. However, when B considers the second priority garnishment it is clear that the amount garnished for child support does not exceed the limit for judicial debt garnishment. ($40 is less than $93.75) B must, therefore, deduct $53.75 for the second priority garnishment. This second deduction cannot be larger because the sum of both garnishments must equal the judicial debt garnishment limit of $93.75.

If, in our examples, A had a third lower priority garnishment, B would go on and consider paying it. B could deduct for this garnishment only if the sum of all garnishment deductions was less than the limit for the third priority garnishment.

Special Considerations

Out of State Garnishment Orders

Generally, garnishment orders of state courts and state agencies outside Indiana do not have the force of law in Indiana. (There are exceptions to this rule for Child Support Deduction Orders and Spouse Support Deduction Orders, and also for a garnishment order issued by a state student loan guaranty agency of any state, provided that it invokes the authority of federal law.) Subject to these exceptions, an Indiana employer must refuse to obey a garnishment order issued by a non-Indiana state court or state agency. Such out-of-state orders must be "domesticated" by an Indiana court. When a creditor secures domestication, the result will be a judicial Debt Garnishment Order issued by an Indiana court. This domesticated order must, then, be obeyed.

As a general rule, employers should refuse to respond to garnishment interrogatories received from courts in other states, until they have consulted legal counsel. A very significant exception to this rule is that all Child Support Deduction Orders and Spouse Support Deduction Orders issued by courts of other states or authorized family support agencies in other states have the full force of law in Indiana. The Indiana General Assembly has enacted legislation giving full force to such support orders as if they were issued by Indiana courts or agencies. There is no need for such orders to be domesticated or even registered in Indiana.

Pre-Order Wage Garnishment in Indiana

The courts of Indiana have created a confusing rule concerning the initiation of wage garnishment for judicial wage garnishment proceedings. Under this rule an employer must initiate wage garnishment as soon as the employer receives notice that the garnishor is *attempting* to garnish the employee's wages. Usually, this notice will consist of a summons, mailed or handed to the employer, along with a questionnaire bearing the title "Interrogatories." There is no clear standard for how quickly withholding must begin after receipt of notice. However, some local courts in Indiana have held employers liable for funds they failed to deduct when a summons was received on the day before payday.

This requirement to withhold wages prior to entry of an order places the employer in a difficult position, because the garnishor is not yet entitled to receive the money withheld. That entitlement only arises when the court issues a garnishment order. That order may not be entered for a period of weeks or months. During that interval, the employer must withhold and retain the monies deducted from wages. Obviously, the employer must insure that these deductions are safeguarded and accounted for. When the order is finally issued, the full amount should be paid to the clerk of the court. If the action is dismissed without entry of an order, and the dismissal is positively verified, the employer should return the deductions to the employee.

Any delay in initiating withholding can be costly. If the garnishor follows through and obtains a wage garnishment order, and the employee then quits or files a bankruptcy petition, the employer will be required to pay to the garnishor the amount it should have withheld.

Fees for Performing Garnishment

An employer cannot be reimbursed for the administrative expense of making deductions pursuant to a Bankruptcy Wage Deduction Order, an IRS Tax Levy, a Spouse Support Deduction Order or a Student Loan Default Garnishment. However, some reimbursement is available for Child Support Deduction Orders and Judicial Debt Garnishment Orders.

In the case of a Child Support Deduction Order, an employer is entitled to deduct a fee of $2 from the employee's wages each time the deduction is made for support. In the case of a judicial Debt Garnishment Order, the employer is entitled to a one-time fee of the greatest of (1) three percent of the amount to be garnished, or (2) $12. Half of the fee is deducted from the employee's wages, while the other half is deducted from the amount paid to the court.

Employee Bankruptcy

The employer must immediately stop all garnishments if the employee files a bankruptcy petition. A bankruptcy filing initiates an automatic stay that prohibits all collection action against the debtor-employee. This stay remains in effect until the employee's bankruptcy case ends in dismissal or discharge. In some cases, a Child Support Deduction Order or a Spouse Support Deduction Order may be paid even while the stay is in effect. However, no deductions of any kind should be made after notice of a bankruptcy filing without advice of legal counsel.

Employee Disputes with the Garnishor

If the employee feels that a garnishment order is invalid, the employee's dispute must be addressed directly to the issuing court or agency. The employer is not a party to such a dispute and should begin deduction in compliance with the garnishment order.

Garnishment from Lump Sums

As a general rule, any category of wage garnishment order does not apply to lump sum payments such as bonuses, performance awards or severance pay. Wage garnishment orders usually authorize deductions only from wages, salaries and commissions. However, some garnishment orders will be specifically worded to require deductions from lump sums as well. Employers owing lump sums to an employee under a wage garnishment order should review the wording of the order and seek legal advice.

Discharge of Employee as a Result of Garnishment

Indiana law prohibits discharge of an employee as a result of a garnishment. This prohibition applies no matter how many garnishments an employee receives. An employer should not discharge an employee if the existence of one or more wage garnishments plays any role at all in the termination decision.

Deductions from Worker's Compensation Awards

Worker's compensation awards are generally exempt from judicial garnishment orders (including orders to collect Indiana taxes), spouse support orders and child support orders. However, Indiana law permits a limited exception. Worker's compensation awards for temporary total disability and permanent total disability are subject to withholding for child support (but not spouse support or other garnishments), subject to two limitations. First, the maximum amount subject to withholding for support orders still applies. Second, the amount withheld from the worker's compensation award may never exceed one-half of the compensation award. Indiana law does not permit withholding from benefits for temporary partial disability or permanent partial disability.

In theory, any order issued under federal authority seeking garnishment of a worker's compensation award pre-empts Indiana law and is enforceable. In the event of such a federal garnishment of a worker's compensation award, an employer should contact the garnishment authority and consult legal counsel.

Voluntary Deductions

Voluntary deductions from pay such as contributions to retirement plans and repayment of debts to the employer or to a credit union are a part of disposable earnings. Such voluntary deductions are made only after all valid garnishment deductions have been made.

Table Showing Garnishment Characteristics

Summary Table of Garnishment Characteristics							
Wage Garnishment Category	**Bankruptcy Wage Deduction Order**	**Child Support Deduction Order**	**IRS Tax Levy**	**Spouse Support Deduction Order**	**Judgment Debt Garnishment Order**	**Indiana Tax Garnishment**	**Student Loan Default Garnishment Order**
Relative Priority	1	2/4**	3	5	5	5	5
Issuing Court or Agency	Any U.S. Bankruptcy Court.	Court of family support agency of any state.	IRS	Court of family support agency of any state.	Any Indiana court.	Any Indiana court, the sheriff of any Indiana county or the Indiana Department of Revenue.	The U.S. Department of Education or any state student loan guaranty agency.
Out-of-State Orders Valid?	Yes. Orders of any U.S. bankruptcy court is valid in Indiana.	Yes. Order of any state court or family support agency is valid in Indiana.	Yes. Order of IRS is valid.	Yes. Order of any state court or family support agency is valid in Indiana.	No. Any order of an out-of-state court must be domesticated before an Indiana court.	No. Any order of an out-of-state court or agency must be domesticated before an Indiana court.	Yes. Any order from the Department of Education or a guaranty agency is valid in Indiana.
Employer Begins Deduction	On receipt of order.	On receipt of order.	On receipt of levy.	On receipt of order.	On receipt of notice. However, funds should not be transferred to court until receipt of order.	On receipt of notice. However, funds should not be transferred to court until receipt of order.	On receipt of order.
Employer Authorized to Collect Fee?	No.	Yes.	No.	No.	Yes.	Yes.	No.
Garnishment Limit	None. Bankruptcy court may garnish all wages except deductions for federal, state and local taxes.	Limit 1. (See Limit Table)	Limit 2. (See Limit Table)	Limit 1. (See Limit Table)	Limit 3. (See Limit Table)	Limit 3. (See Limit Table)	Limit 3 and Limit 4. (See Limit Table)
Remarks	Order usually bars all other garnishments. Some orders may permit only Child Support Garnishment.						

** The priority of a Child Support Deduction Order is above the priority of an IRS Tax Levy if the Child Support Deduction Order is dated earlier than the levy. Otherwise the levy has highest priority.

Limit Table

Limit Table		
The following deduction limits apply to the garnishment categories as indicated.		
LIMIT NUMBER	**APPLICABLE TO**	**DETERMINATION RULE**
LIMIT 1	Child Support Deduction Order. Spouse Support Deduction Order.	The amount to be deducted is the lesser of (1) the dollar amount specified in the support order, and (2) the maximum support order deduction allowed by federal and Indiana law. The formulas used to determine the maximum allowable deduction are as follows: (a) If the employee is supporting a current spouse or dependent child and is ordered to support an ex-spouse or different dependent child, 50 percent of weekly disposable earnings can be taken; (b) If the employee is not currently supporting a spouse or child other than those referred to in the support order, then 60 percent of disposable earnings can be taken; (c) In either case (50 percent or 60 percent), an additional five percent of the disposable earnings can be taken for arrearages more than 12 weeks old. As a general rule, employers should use the 60 percent deduction limit. It is up to the court to inform the employer if the employee is in arrears requiring an extra five percent deduction. It is up to the employee to convince the court that support of current dependants merits use of the 50 percent deduction. The term "disposable income" is defined in Appendix A.
LIMIT 2	IRS Tax Levy.	The amount to be deducted is all of the employee's disposable income except the exempt pay determined by reference to IRS Publication 1494. NO DEDUCTION MAY BE GREATER THAN THE TOTAL REMAINING DEBT OWED BY THE EMPLOYEE.
LIMIT 3	Judgment Debt Garnishment Order. Indiana Tax Garnishment. Student Loan Default Garnishment Order.	The amount to be deducted is determined by a formula established by both Indiana and federal law. For any workweek, the employer must withhold the lesser of: (a) Twenty-five percent of the employee's disposable earnings; or (b) that amount by which the employee's disposable earnings exceeds 30 times the federal minimum hourly wage. The federal minimum wage is currently $5.15 and, thus, this exempt amount is $154.50 per week. For pay periods other than the week, subrule (b), above, is modified proportionally. NO DEDUCTION MAY BE GREATER THAN THE TOTAL REMAINING DEBT OWED BY THE EMPLOYEE.
LIMIT 4	Student Loan Default Garnishment Order.	The amount to be deducted may not exceed 10 percent of the employee's disposable earnings. NO DEDUCTION MAY BE GREATER THAN THE TOTAL REMAINING DEBT OWED BY THE EMPLOYEE.

Index

employment certificates required, 137-138
Employment Standards Administration, 141, 158, 160
engaged to wait, 61
enterprise coverage, 7-9
enterprise test, single coverage, 16-17
equal effort, 173
Equal Employment Opportunity Commission (EEOC), 169, 176
Equal Pay Act (EPA), 169-177
  background, 169
  elements of violation, 170-173
  employees covered, 170
  enforcement and remedies under, 176-177
  exceptions to, 173-176
  requirements, 169-170
equal responsibility, 173
equal skill, 172-173
escrow/mortgage closers, 45
Evansville, 142
exception to hours restriction, 134
exceptions to EPA requirements, 173-176
exceptions to single workweek rule, 84-85
exclusions from regular rate of pay, 95-96
executive assistants, 45
executive equity owners, 21
executive exemptions, 20-21
executive secretaries, 45
exempt pay, 180
exemptions, 19-57
  commissioned sales people, 55-56
  computer occupational professional, 46-48
  deductions, 49-51
  motor carrier act exemption, 54
  outside sales exemption, 51-53
  proposed regulations to change exemptions, 57
  salary basis requirement, 49
  seasonal amusements and recreation establishments, 56
  white collar exemptions, 20-45
extra compensation, 96
exempt employees, 113

F

FLSA, *see* Fair Labor Standards Act
FMLA, *see* Family and Medical Leave Act
facility use, 121
Fair Labor Standards Act (FLSA), 1-3, 142-147
  coverage under, 5-18

civil litigation under, 148-154
enterprise coverage, 7-9
illegal aliens covered by, 18
independent contractors, 9-15
individual employee, 5-7
joint employment, 15
single enterprise test, 16-17
volunteers, 17-18
Family and Medical Leave Act (FMLA), 49-50, 141, 144
family farm exemption, 136
federal laws and regulations, 157-163
  Davis-Bacon Act, 162-163
  McNamara-O'Hara Service Contract Act, 159-162
  Walsh-Healy Public Contracts Act, 157-159
federal postings, 124
Federal Register, 129
fees for performing garnishments, 194-195
Federal Rules of Civil Procedure, 148
fines prohibited, 79
fixed salary for fixed hours, 97-101
fixed salary for fluctuating hours, 101-103
fluctuating hours overtime agreement, 102
Fort Wayne, 142
fourteen-day work period, 117

G

gap time, compensated and non-compensated, 97-100
garnishment of wages, 179-198,
  categories of wage garnishment, 182-188
  glossary of terms, 180
  introduction, 179
  invalid wage garnishment orders, 188-189
  multiple garnishments, 189-192
  special considerations, 193-196
  wage garnishment, 181-182
Gary, 142
general requirements for recordkeeping and posting, 112-114
  child labor, 114
  exempt employees, 113
  minors, 114
  non-exempt employees, 112-113
gifts, 95

Walsh-Healy Public Contracts Act, 2-3,
    157-159
    minimum wage and overtime
        requirements, 158
    notice to employees, 159
    prime contractors, 159
    prohibited employment, 159
    safety provisions, 158
Walling v. Portland Terminal Company,
    330 U.S. 148 (1947), 65
weekly pay and payroll certification, 165
weighted average rate, 87-89, 165
white collar exemptions, 20-45
    defining the administrative
        exemption, 22-23
    defining the executive exemption, 20-
        21
    defining the professional exemption,
        23-25
    determining whether an exemption
        applies, 34-45
    executive equity owners, 21
    motor carrier act exemption, 31-33
    outside sales exemption, 25-31
    proposed regulations to change
        exemption qualifications,
    seasonal amusement and recreation
        establishment, 33-34
window of correction, 50
Wisconsin, 141
work incentive bonuses, 90
worker's compensation awards, 196
working time, compensable, 59-70
workweek, determination of, 83-90
    calculating the regular rate of pay, 85-
    90
exceptions to the single workweek rule,
    84-85

We keep our promises to you

To learn more about the company that has been insuring responsible drivers since 1907, call the **Indianapolis Office** at **800-24-AMICA.** Or visit us at **amica.com** and experience *a company that actually does what it promises.*